In the manner of a shrewd war tactician, Bishop George Bloomer has uncovered the satanic psychological operations of the wicked deceiver and his ploy to turn man from God. The principles in *Spiritual Warfare* allow the body of Christ to take an out-of-body view of itself in order to surgically detach it from the world system's mind-set. I thank God for raising a spiritual leader like Bishop Bloomer. From the moment Bishop sat to pen this book, Satan began rolling in anguish. Each page turned by a saint is a dagger into his diabolical heart.

—*Bishop Eddie L. Long*
*Senior Pastor*
*New Birth Missionary Baptist Church*
*Lithonia, Georgia*

After perusing *Spiritual Warfare*, two things became very clear to me. First, it is very obvious that George Bloomer is on a divine assignment to lift the lid off the strategies of the enemy so that all believers can live a life of power and victory. Second, because of George Bloomer's faithfulness to this assignment, hell is turning over and Satan has been forced back to the drawing board. Every believer who is serious about canceling the agenda of Satan over his life ought to read this book.

—*Bishop Neil C. Ellis*
*Senior Pastor*
*Mount Tabor Full Gospel Baptist Church*
*Nassau, Bahamas*

In *Spiritual Warfare*, Bishop George Bloomer has presented a balanced, reasoned approach to the often abused and controversial topic of spiritual warfare. He employs his considerable teaching gift to provide solid and substantive strategies for believers, that they might capably and intelligently *"contend for the faith which was once delivered unto the saints"* (Jude 1:3 KJV).

—*Pastor Jacqueline E. McCullough*
*Senior Pastor*
*The Gathering at Beth Rapha*
*Pomona, New York*

*Spiritual Warfare* is a book that guarantees to expose the forces of the enemy and eliminate his agenda in the lives of those who believe and receive. George Bloomer's divine insight and lucid stratagems on defeating the enemy will impel readers to rise and fight the good fight of faith, war against the enemy, and intercept Satan's weapons of destruction. A book designed to impart and provoke positive reaction, *Spiritual Warfare* is the type of supernatural armament needed in the body of Christ to incapacitate Lucifer's armed forces!

—*Bishop Noel Jones*
*Senior Pastor*
*Greater Bethany Community Church*
*Los Angeles, California*

# SPIRITUAL Warfare

# SPIRITUAL Warfare

## GEORGE BLOOMER

ω
WHITAKER
HOUSE

This is a revised and expanded version of the original text, *This Is War*. Material from the following titles has been included:
*The Witching Craft* (ISBN: 1-89235-208-7)
*Weapons for Warriors* (ISBN: 1-89235-230-3)
Permission to quote from these sources has been granted by G. G. Bloomer Ministries.

---

**SPIRITUAL WARFARE** ·
*(Expanded version of the previously published title, This Is War)*

ISBN: 0-88368-683-X
Printed in the United States of America
© 2001, 2004 by George Bloomer

Whitaker House
30 Hunt Valley Circle
New Kensington, PA 15068
website: www.whitakerhouse.com

---

**Library of Congress Cataloging-in-Publication Data**

Bloomer, George G., 1963–
Spiritual warfare / George Bloomer.— Rev. and expanded ed.
p.  cm.
Rev. ed. of: This is war. © 2001.
ISBN 0-88368-683-X (pbk. : alk. paper)
1. Spiritual warfare. I. Bloomer, George G., 1963– This is war.
II. Title.
BV4509.5.B57 2004
235'.4—dc22
2003026569

2  3  4  5  6  7  8  9  10  **ᵾ**  10  09  08  07  06  05  04

# Contents

# Introduction

I was raised in the projects of Brooklyn, New York. We lived on the sixth floor of a government building in apartments A, B, and C, so we had a "condo in the ghetto." We were raised on welfare, food stamps, government cheese, and Buster Brown shoes. If you could wear out a pair of Buster Brown shoes, you were *bad*! I grew up in a household that at one time included twenty-four children and, therefore, constant struggles for territory. From who got the last piece of pie to whose shoes you were wearing, there always was a battle going on and a pecking order being established.

We kids employed many strategies in this battle. Sometimes a strategy was so subtle the rest of us were hardly aware that anything was happening. You could call this the "I'll manage you" maneuver. Some waged war using the "I'll scare you" maneuver, engendering fear among the other children. Occasionally those who were able used the "I'll crush you" maneuver, where only the strong survive and the mighty slay the weak. Whatever the method, the battle raged on with frequent skirmishes.

Everyone had his or her own turf—and a strategy to maintain it. I had a brother who turned the "I'll trick you" maneuver into an art form. He was younger and smaller than most, so the option of threat or brute force was not available to him. But he knew how to whine and how to push the right buttons to get what he wanted. He used his small size as a strategy: He threw tantrums. He was able to use the family members' own love against them.

My brother would show his displeasure in rages of self-destructive fury, getting red in the face and stomping his feet until my parents thought he would explode. Needless to say, he frequently got what he wanted and so maintained his turf. He was a champion *manipulator.* He was able to manage the family as if he were ten feet tall.

Unfortunately, what began as voluntary fits of self-will later became physical affliction. Satan was able to capitalize on my brother's manipulative antics and turned his tantrums into seizures, which ultimately caused him to go into a coma. And it all started through manipulation—his manipulating my mom and the rest of the family to get what he wanted.

This same war is fought on every level of humanity. It is fought in the family, on school playgrounds, in corporate headquarters, and even among nations. In each case the strategies remain the same. We of the household of God must realize that this same warfare is going on in the church. Hell-inspired maneuvers are being executed all around us. Battles are fought and demonic strategies employed from the front door to the pastor's study to the choir loft.

These attacks are the product of a deliberate, demonic strategy. There is a war being waged in us and through us, and we are all caught up in it. It is a war wrought from rebellion around the highest throne of heaven.

We are talking about spiritual warfare in this book, but we will approach it in a more personal way than you may have considered. We will discover how to unmask the strategies of the enemy and how to free ourselves from his devices—and we will learn how to live a life of power from the throne of God Himself. These are the issues we will take up in this book. It's about *you*...it's about your *family*...it's about your *church*.

This is war, but we are the victors in Christ Jesus!

*And they overcame him by the blood of the Lamb and by the word of their testimony, and they did not love their lives to the death. Therefore rejoice, O heavens, and you who dwell in them! Woe to the inhabitants of the earth and the sea! For the devil has come down to you, having great wrath, because he knows that he has a short time.* (Revelation 12:11–12)

# Chapter One

## Rebellion at the Throne of God

## Chapter One

# Rebellion at the Throne of God

*You were the seal of perfection, full of wisdom and perfect in beauty. You were in Eden, the garden of God; every precious stone was your covering: the sardius, topaz, and diamond, beryl, onyx, and jasper, sapphire, turquoise, and emerald with gold. The workmanship of your timbrels and pipes was prepared for you on the day you were created. You were the anointed cherub who covers; I established you; you were on the holy mountain of God; you walked back and forth in the midst of fiery stones. You were perfect in your ways from the day you were created, till iniquity was found in you.*
—Ezekiel 28:12–15

## SOMEWHERE BEFORE TIME

Before there was time—before there was anything—he was the brightest of the brilliant, the highest of the exalted. He stood at the throne of the Most High, consumed in its glory. All that surrounded him burned with the holy intensity of the presence of God. He was perfection; his beauty was such that it can scarcely be described by the tongues of men. His appearance was as thousands of precious stones of every hue and color, refracting and magnifying the unapproachable light of the Creator. He was the personification of worship itself, covering the very throne of God. His worship was the reflection of God's glory.

To him was given wisdom and authority above all others. He stood at the place of ultimate influence in heaven. He was the joy of his Creator—a being created for adoration and given a place at the apex of all that there was. He was Lucifer, the morning star, the supreme servant of God.

## A MOMENT'S GLANCE

Somewhere in the vastness of eternity, the anointed cherub was distracted from his worship of the Sovereign of heaven and caught a fleeting glance of his own image. His heart was filled with the wonder of his own appearance. He beheld his own beauty for an instant—and changed eternity. Though he had all wisdom and authority, it would never again be enough.

He coveted the worship and honor of heaven. In that momentary deflection of adoration, the crookedness of iniquity was born in him. He said in his heart,

*I will ascend into heaven, I will exalt my throne above the stars of God; I will also sit on the mount of the congregation on the farthest sides of the north; I will ascend above the heights of the clouds, I will be like the Most High.*      (Isaiah 14:13–14, emphasis added)

Lucifer's priority shifted from reflecting the glory of God in worship to seeking glory for himself. This one who had stood at the place of ultimate influence at the throne of God perverted his position, lusting after the adoration that filled heaven. He took his eyes off his Creator and sought his own glory. He thought, *I can be just like God!* And, turning his eyes from God for an instant, he lost all.

He who was exalted was now cast down—fallen below the others whose devotion was stayed on the throne of God. Now, this son of the morning, this brilliant cherub, would be banished to lesser domains, to lesser lights.

There were others who were fascinated with Lucifer. They diverted their focus from the throne of God and became converts to mutiny. Perhaps as many as a third of heaven's warring host joined Lucifer and was cast down with him.

*And war broke out in heaven: Michael and his angels fought with the dragon; and the dragon and his angels*

*fought, but they did not prevail, nor was a place found for them in heaven any longer. So the great dragon was cast out, that serpent of old, called the Devil and Satan, who deceives the whole world; he was cast to the earth, and his angels were cast out with him.*

(Revelation 12:7–9)

And there was a void in heaven—a chasm of adoration to be filled.

# IT'S ALL ABOUT INFLUENCE

All that happened at the throne of God, all that resulted in separation and war, was tied up in one word: *influence*. Lucifer, or Satan, was at the pinnacle of influence in heaven. The purpose of heaven was worship of God, and Lucifer was the instigator of worship. In a primordial instant, Lucifer turned away from God, and iniquity was born.

> THE PURPOSE OF HEAVEN WAS WORSHIP OF GOD.

The Hebrew word for iniquity, *avon*, denotes a crookedness, a perversity.\* It specifically indicates a turning or a deflection in another direction. In heaven everything was flowing toward the throne of God in worship. There could be no other direction, no other object worthy of praise. Then came a change in course: Lucifer deflected his worship away from God and onto himself. As a result,

---

\* *Strong's Exhaustive Concordance of the Bible* (Iowa Falls: World Bible Publishers, Inc., 1980, 1986), H#5771.

18

the peace of heaven was shattered. (Isaiah 26:3 says, "*You will keep him in perfect peace, whose mind is stayed on You.*")

This diversion, this other, less worthy self-worship, is the very definition of iniquity. It is a diversion from God or the ways of God. Iniquity has been Satan's nature and diversion his strategy since creation. He uses whatever he can to influence us away from God.

Consider the events surrounding the fall of man. Lucifer exchanged his eternal beauty for the skin of a snake and slithered into the Paradise of God. He left his place in the *adoration* to God and took up a place in the *accusation* of man, hence his name change to Satan, the accuser.

Satan saw man enjoying God's attention and fellowship as they visited in the cool of the day. Man stood in the place of intimacy that Lucifer had lost. Now Lucifer sought to bring down the new object of God's affection: man. Note Satan's words to Eve:

> *Then the serpent said to the woman, "You will not surely die. For God knows that in the day you eat of it your eyes will be opened, and you will be like God, knowing good and evil."*  (Genesis 3:4–5)

Does this sound familiar? What Satan was saying to Eve was an echo of what he said to himself, that he could be "just like God." Satan told Eve, "*You will be like God,*" and for an instant Eve believed him and disobeyed God. Now man was infected with the disease of iniquity, the crookedness inspired by Satan.

The devil is all about influence. His desire is to have us take our eyes off God and put them on ourselves. Notice that he was filled with *"I will"* as he fell. The issue was not what *God* willed, but what *he* willed. Our enemy encourages and influences us to move into this same self-willed way. We are more concerned about *"I will"* than about God's will. So we spend our lives, inside and outside the church, getting what *we will*. This leads us toward all kinds of man-centered doctrines and strategies for personal gain. However, *whatever serves to enrich us at the expense of God's glory is iniquity.*

There is a war being waged in the heavenlies for our minds and hearts. The devil and his minions of fallen demonic servants are at work on us, in us, and through us. If they can, Satan's host will divert us from giving glory to God and cause us to believe that we are not as close to Him as we think we are. They assist us in getting *our wills* accomplished—in pleasing our carnality.

The result is that our personal lives, our families, and our churches have become spiritual war zones. Most of the time, however, we are ignorant of the war raging around us. In fact, we believe that conflict and sin are normal. We even jockey for position within the community of God's people and think nothing of trampling a brother or sister under the feet of our ecclesiastical ambitions. We defend our turf, and we lose sight of God in the process.

Satan lost his place and wants us to lose ours as well. He is much like a jealous woman who sees another woman enjoying an "old flame" of hers. Satan hates to see the loving relationship between God and His saints and does everything in his power to destroy it. The very thought of God's creation enjoying any part of what Satan once enjoyed himself deeply angers him, and like a jealous woman trying to rip apart a relationship that she wishes she could have, Satan seeks to destroy the love and fellowship God and has with His saints.

THOSE WHO HAVE ACCEPTED GOD'S GRACE CANNOT BE SEPARATED FROM HIM.

The reality is that those who have accepted the grace of God through Jesus Christ cannot be separated from Him. As Paul wrote,

> Who shall separate us from the love of Christ? Shall tribulation, or distress, or persecution, or famine, or nakedness, or peril, or sword? As it is written: "For Your sake we are killed all day long; we are accounted as sheep for the slaughter." Yet in all these things we are more than conquerors through Him who loved us. For I am persuaded that neither death nor life, nor angels nor principalities nor powers, nor things present nor things to come, nor height nor depth, nor any other created thing, shall be able to separate us from the love of God which is in Christ Jesus our Lord. (Romans 8:35–39)

## SATAN'S POWER SOURCE

A very basic yet important question we must ask is: Where did Satan get the power he is using to deceive and enslave mankind? The answer is: from God Almighty.

Next we might ask: Why does God allow the devil to have such power? Perhaps the best way to reach an understanding of this question is to refer to Adam and Eve's transgression in Genesis 2:16–17.

*And the* Lord *God commanded the man, saying, "Of every tree of the garden you may freely eat; but of the tree of the knowledge of good and evil you shall not eat, for in the day that you eat of it you shall surely die."*

Of course, Adam and Eve did disobey and ate from the Tree of Knowledge of Good and Evil. Because they did, we, as their offspring, also have a knowledge of good and evil and a nature that strays toward evil. Since God is good and there is no evil in Him (see James 1:13, 17), He cannot tolerate the evil in us. He has allowed the devil to continue to exist to show us the difference between good and evil to help us make a proper choice.

*See, I have set before you today life and good, death and evil....I call heaven and earth as witnesses today against you, that I have set before you life and death, blessing and cursing; therefore choose life, that both you and your descendants may live.*
(Deuteronomy 30:15, 19)

Although Satan has power, the book of Job reveals that he is under God's authority and that God can limit and prevent his attacks. (See Job 1:6–12.) This is because God has sovereignty and truly holds the reins, not Satan. Nothing can be done apart from Him.

# A POWERFUL ILLUSION

Satan wants to make us believe that he has power. And he does. But his power is tied up in heaven's legal system. He can't use it any way he'd like to because he's held in check by God, who has our interests in mind.

A good example of this is a will. I could die tomorrow, leaving all my money to the benefactors of my will. But if other members of my family wanted to, they could contest my will in favor of their own interests. This would then lock up my willed money until my rightful heirs got a lawyer and straightened things out. Those wanting to alter my will would probably try to prove the unjustness of my choice. But once my heirs got a good lawyer on the case, the legality of my will would defeat their arguments.

Similarly, God has willed salvation and blessings to those who receive His saving grace. But Satan has contested the will of God. As a result, you have to petition your advocate, Jesus, to take him on. But Jesus has never lost a case! He will seal your court papers with drops of His sacrificial blood and the case will be closed.

You see, no matter how powerful Satan seems to be, he is nowhere near as powerful as our Lord. So many believers have this notion—whether they realize it or not—that Satan is equal in power to God. They have what could be called a Star Wars view of spiritual things. Just as there is a "light side" and an equally powerful "dark side" to the Force in the Star Wars movies, these Christians think there is a "light side" (God) and an equally powerful "dark side" (Satan) that make up the cosmos. This is not biblical!

Although Satan retained his intelligence and power after the Fall, his power never did and never can exceed the power of almighty God. Satan may have knowledge, but he is the greatest fool of all. No matter how powerful Satan may seem, He is under divine control and cannot do anything outside of God's permissive will.

Satan may have caused the Fall, but he is not all-powerful. We must understand this as we engage in spiritual warfare. We must always remember that Satan is already defeated!

SATAN IS NOT ALL-POWERFUL. ALL DOMINION BELONGS TO GOD.

However, although the devil is not all-powerful, he can still influence us. He can tempt us, mislead us, and even make us believe that we are separated from God. This is his tool for robbing God of His rightful worship. And this is how he diminishes our effectiveness in the kingdom of God.

We must always remember two things when we're dealing with the topic of spiritual warfare:

1. Satan is not all powerful. All power and dominion belongs to God and God alone.

2. Although Satan is not all powerful, he can still influence us so that our lives are marked by disobedience and rebellion to God.

24

It's important that we remember both of these points. We can't give Satan too much credit, but we can't ignore him either. It's our responsibility, aided by guidance from the Holy Spirit, to keep these two in balance.

Now that we know why Satan does what he does, let's spend some time learning how he does it. It is only when we are equipped with knowledge that we will be able to fight him effectively.

> *Be sober, be vigilant; because your adversary the devil walks about like a roaring lion, seeking whom he may devour. Resist him, steadfast in the faith, knowing that the same sufferings are experienced by your brother- hood in the world. But may the God of all grace, who called us to His eternal glory by Christ Jesus, after you have suffered a while, perfect, establish, strengthen, and settle you. To Him be the glory and the dominion forever and ever. Amen.* (1 Peter 5:8–11)

# Chapter Two

# Living under the Influence

# Chapter Two

---

# Living under
# the Influence

Several years ago, I read a book that dealt with the incredible violence that has occurred in the United States Postal Service. At regular intervals, disturbed former postal employees fired upon post offices, killing and wounding many people. The reasons given for these massacres seem to be trivial when compared to the carnage that results. Is it mere coincidence that post office massacres were so common? Apparently not.

According to the book, the events described were the result of a curse. The book revealed that, sometime in the early twentieth century, people dressed in witches' garb gathered to pronounce a curse on the United States Postal Service. What happened in these post offices was no mere coincidence. It was the result of a deliberate act of witchcraft.

# WITCHCRAFT

> WITCHCRAFT OPERATES ALL AROUND US WHETHER WE ARE AWARE OF IT OR NOT.

Normally, when we think of witchcraft, we envision black cats and old hags dressed in black with pointy hats and riding on broomsticks. In reality, however, witchcraft is an attempt to influence someone by ungodly spiritual means. It is the calling forth of spiritual influences with the goal of causing someone or something to perform in a certain way. Witchcraft is bringing a person or a thing under the influence of the demonic.

What exactly are demons? Demons are those angels who were cast out of heaven with Lucifer. *Demonology* is the understanding of how these evil influences work and act. In short, demonic forces operate according to a deliberate satanic strategy to influence people and events, diverting worship and devotion away from God. Witchcraft was a factor in the Bible, and it is a factor that operates all around us today, though we are scarcely aware of it.

In order to deal with the reality of witchcraft, we first must understand some basic truths. The first truth is that we are not just dealing with human weakness and peculiarity. We are dealing with spiritual forces bent on our destruction.

> *For we are not fighting against people made of flesh and blood, but against persons without bodies — the evil rulers of the unseen world, those mighty satanic beings and great evil princes of darkness who rule this world; and against huge numbers of wicked spirits in the spirit world.* (Ephesians 6:12 TLB)

We are a nation living under the influence of witchcraft: the witchcraft of the occult, the witchcraft of drugs, the witchcraft of religious spirits, and the witchcraft of rebellion. Regardless of the method or the venue, evil influences stem from the same source: Satan. And all have the same motive, which is to divert people from God and His truth. Now, I am not saying that all of the evil things that happen can be ascribed to Satan; that would give him too much power and glory. Nonetheless, witchcraft influences us in many forms and guises.

# THE WITCHCRAFT OF THE OCCULT

There are many gateways through which deliberate satanic influence enters into our world. One of them is the occult. For example, there are advertisements everywhere for psychic hot lines, where desperate people consult demonically controlled counselors over the telephone.

Both the Old and the New Testaments in the Bible contain examples of occult witchcraft. In fact, God was very clear about avoiding divination of any sort:

*Give no regard to mediums and familiar spirits; do not seek after them, to be defiled by them: I am the Lord your God.* (Leviticus 19:31)

and,

*And the person who turns to mediums and familiar spirits, to prostitute himself with them, I will set My face against that person and cut him off from his people.* (Leviticus 20:6)

and,

*There shall not be found among you anyone who makes his son or his daughter pass through the fire, or one who practices witchcraft, or a soothsayer, or one who interprets omens, or a sorcerer, or one who conjures spells, or a medium, or a spiritist, or one who calls up the dead. For all who do these things are an abomination to the Lord.* (Deuteronomy 18:10–12)

The central issue in the prohibition of sorcery in the Old Testament was that it led people away from God and attempted to control future events through spells and evil spirits. Again, the result was separation from God. God warned Israel about taking up the gods and altars of the people they were to displace in the Promised Land.

*When the LORD your God brings you into the land which you go to possess, and has cast out many nations before you, the Hittites and the Girgashites and the Amorites and the Canaanites and the Perizzites and the Hivites and the Jebusites, seven nations greater and mightier than you, and when the LORD your God delivers them over to you, you shall conquer them and utterly destroy them. You shall make no covenant with them nor show mercy to them. Nor shall you make marriages with them. You shall not give your daughter to their son, nor take their daughter for your son. For they will turn your sons away from following Me, to serve other gods; so the anger of the LORD will be aroused against you and destroy you suddenly. But thus you shall deal with them: you shall destroy their altars, and break down their sacred pillars, and cut down their wooden images, and burn their carved images with fire.*

(Deuteronomy 7:1–5)

The people of God were warned not to get involved in any way with those who did not serve God. They were to tear down and destroy the enemy influences among them. We know from reading the rest of the Scriptures that the Israelites did not do so. The nations that God displaced served false gods of every sort, and some of their occult practices crept unnoticed into the everyday lives of God's people.

The Israelites had been desert wanderers and shepherds for many years, and slaves before that. But when they came into the land of promise, they had to become farmers. Being unfamiliar with the ways of farming, they probably picked up pagan practices by observation. Perhaps a pagan farmer placed a small idol at the end of his field to ensure a good crop. The Israelites then saw that idol as just something everybody did to get good crops, so they set up idols too. In doing so, though, they placed themselves under the legal control of demonic influence. Thus, little by little, they took up pagan practices until God became just one god among many. Second Kings 17 says, *"They feared the LORD, yet served their own gods; according to the rituals of the nations from among whom they were carried away"* (verse 33).

Superstition, New Age, and occult practices have crept into the church as well. Though some may be offended at what I'm about to say, I must caution some African-American churches that have taken up the celebration of Kwanza.

## OCCULT PRACTICES HAVE EVEN CREPT INTO THE CHURCH.

This holiday is supposed to be a celebration of African culture and is filled with color and ritual. But it also is filled with demonic influence. Kwanza is rooted in an African religion that is polluted with spiritism. The name *Kwanza* comes from the Swahili words for "firstfruits," and it is a harvest celebration that dates back as far as ancient Egypt. Kwanza does not glorify Yahweh God in any way. Those who celebrate this holiday unknowingly serve pagan false gods. There can be no mixture in the kingdom of God. God alone is worthy to be worshiped and adored. We cannot fear the Lord and at the same time serve other gods in any form or to any extent.

Similarly, in very subtle ways, the church has taken up the gods of materialism from the world that we are supposed to be claiming for Christ. Celebrity preachers wear thousand-dollar suits and drive sixty-thousand-dollar cars. We have placed ourselves under the demonic influence of materialism and have learned to measure our success in terms of facilities and dollars. How are we different from drug dealers? Jesus set a different standard for His disciples.

> *And when Jesus saw great multitudes about Him, He gave a command to depart to the other side. Then a certain scribe came and said to Him, "Teacher, I will follow You wherever You go." And Jesus said to him, "Foxes have holes and birds of the air have nests, but the Son of Man has nowhere to lay His head."*
> (Matthew 8:18–20)

In the New Testament there are a few notable examples of witchcraft. In Acts 16:16 we read of a slave girl who was controlled by a spirit of divination. Not only did the spirit that oppressed her control her life, this same spirit sought to control or influence others *through* her.

> *Now it happened, as we went to prayer, that a certain slave girl possessed with a spirit of divination met us, who brought her masters much profit by fortune-telling. This girl followed Paul and us, and*

*cried out, saying, "These men are the servants of the Most High God, who proclaim to us the way of salvation." And this she did for many days. But Paul, greatly annoyed, turned and said to the spirit, "I command you in the name of Jesus Christ to come out of her." And he came out that very hour. But when her masters saw that their hope of profit was gone, they seized Paul and Silas and dragged them into the marketplace to the authorities.* (Acts 16:16–19)

Notice that this spirit began its harassment as Paul and the others went to prayer, that place of fellowship with God. Divination is the counterfeit of God's truth. It involves using the stars and evil spirits to foretell or control the future. The girl followed them proclaiming the truth, but in a mocking manner. Finally Paul had had enough and "dispossessed" the demonic spirit in the name of Jesus Christ. We see in the following verse that not only did the spirit influence the girl, but it also brought her masters under the influence of a spirit of greed as they profited by her lying divination. One spirit opened the way for the other. All, however, were living under the influence of the witchcraft of the occult.

In Acts 13:8 Paul had another power encounter with a sorcerer named Elymas.

*But Elymas the sorcerer (for so his name is translated) withstood them, seeking to turn the proconsul away from the faith. Then Saul, who also is called Paul, filled with the Holy Spirit, looked intently at him and said, "O full of all deceit and all fraud, you son of the devil, you enemy of all righteousness, will you not cease perverting the straight ways of the Lord?"*

(Acts 13:8–10)

Note that the man was guilty of diverting others from *"the straight ways of the Lord."* He was employing Satan's old habit of seeking to deflect and distort the true worship of God. Paul also called him a *"son of the devil"*; literally, one who does what the devil does.

In an even earlier account, Peter encountered a sorcerer named Simon who amazed a city of 70,000 people through the power of Satan. But when the people came to Christ, his powers were no longer impressive. So he became a "believer" as well. But did he really? Later, when Simon witnessed the true power of God flowing through Peter, he offered to pay the apostles so that he could have this same power.

> DIVINATION IS THE COUNTERFEIT OF GOD'S TRUTH.

*And when Simon saw that through the laying on of the apostles' hands the Holy Spirit was given, he offered them money, saying, "Give me this power also, that anyone on whom I lay hands may receive the Holy Spirit."*

(Acts 8:18–19)

What was it that Simon offered to purchase? It was power, pure and simple. He had no desire to see the Holy Spirit come upon people to empower them and set them free. It was all about control. Nothing had changed in him; he still wanted to influence and impress. This time it was just through what he saw as a greater power. But the same demonic motive was in operation.

This same spirit is active in the psychic hot lines of today. In many instances these modern soothsayers/ witches are there to tell people what they think they want to hear, while their 900-number meters rack up $3.99 a minute. In all cases the callers are giving legal ground to the enemy to draw them even deeper into the influence of the demonic.

Our nation is living under the influence of the occult in many ways. It is even true that our nation's capitol was designed in the form of the Masonic symbol. The exercises and practices of the Freemasons are filled with the symbols and rites of an ancient Arabic religion, which in some cases glorified the murder of Christians. Its symbols include the inverted pentagram that is also found in witchcraft and Satanism. The Masonic Lodge has been home to many presidents, judges, members of Congress, and other government officials. Nevertheless, the Masonic Lodge, with its secret rites and orders, is an occult organization whose influence is felt throughout every part of the country—even in the church of Jesus Christ.

Whatever the source or description, we are living under the influence of the witchcraft of the occult.

# THE WITCHCRAFT OF DRUGS

Drugs are another tool of the enemy to influence those who use them. Galatians 5:20, in the King James Version, lists witchcraft among the deeds of the flesh.

*Now the works of the flesh are manifest, which are these; adultery, fornication, uncleanness, lasciviousness, idolatry, witchcraft, hatred, variance, emulations, wrath, strife, seditions, heresies, envyings, murders, drunkenness, revellings, and such like.*

(verses 19–21 KJV)

The Greek word used for *"witchcraft"* here is *pharmakeia,** from which we get the word *pharmacy*, the place where prescription drugs are available. In ancient times the pharmacist was one who mixed potions and poisons with which to influence or kill people. Today, illegal drugs enslave us and make us dependent. They waste our lives and our money.

Illegal drugs plague our neighborhoods and families, robbing us of the next generations. At the same time, we must realize that we are also the most medicated people on earth. Never have so many people used prescription drugs. We have drugs to bring us out of depression and drugs to calm our stress. Antidepressant drugs are prescribed almost automatically today. Although in some cases prescription drugs are helpful in correcting chemical imbalances in the brain, that is not the only cause of

---

* *Strong's Exhaustive Concordance of the Bible* (Iowa Falls: World Bible Publishers, Inc., 1980, 1986), G#5331.

depression. Depression also can be the result of demonic influence. Drugs may treat the symptoms, but they fail to address the source of the depression. It is comparable to seeing someone with an arrow stuck in his chest and handing him an aspirin instead of removing the arrow. In any event, drugs of any kind represent a powerful means of influence.

# THE WITCHCRAFT OF RELIGION

Paul asked an interesting question in his epistle to the Galatians. Many in the Galatian church were falling back into a mind-set of works and rituals in order to please those who sought to bind them to religion again. He asked them, *"O foolish Galatians! Who has bewitched you that you should not obey the truth, before whose eyes Jesus Christ was clearly portrayed among you as crucified?"* (Galatians 3:1). It appears that religion itself can be an influencing factor to bring fear into the lives of believers and separate them from the true and living God.

> RELIGION ITSELF CAN BECOME AN OBSTACLE.

What do I mean by *religion*? Religion, in the broadest sense, refers to a system of beliefs about God. But religion itself can become an obstacle if we begin to relate to our system of beliefs or doctrine and forget about our personal relationship with God. For the ancient Jewish people, religion became a mechanical following of rules, done by rote, rather than being motivated by a personal relationship with their God. God Himself told them that, while they practiced religion, their hearts were not in it.

> *Therefore the* LORD *said: "Inasmuch as these people draw near with their mouths and honor Me with their lips, but have removed their hearts far from Me, and their fear toward Me is taught by the commandment of men."* (Isaiah 29:13)

The Galatians had begun to fall back into that religious pattern. They put aside the truth of the Gospel of grace through Jesus Christ and began trying to earn their way to fellowship with God through legalistic religion. If it were possible for us to save ourselves, who would be in control? We would! Man would *"be like God"* (Genesis 3:5). It's the oldest lie in the cosmos. God is God, and He alone saves through His Son Jesus Christ.

Throughout the history of the church, various leaders have tried to exert control over the people they were called to serve. In the Middle Ages, a hierarchy of church leaders evolved that took control of every phase of the people's lives. The church became a political force with the power of life or death. The result was corruption throughout the church to the point of selling forgiveness to those with enough money. Again, those in the church assumed a place that was not theirs. They took their eyes off God and said to themselves, "We can *be like God*" and issue forgiveness. Thankfully, Luther and other Reformers came along, and the church was redirected to its original purpose: worship of God, not a form of religion. (Unfortunately, these

Reformers themselves eventually persecuted those who participated in subsequent reforms.)

It is still a fact, however, that, from time to time, movements and individuals rise up and assume a place of control. Leaders must remain diligent to examine their hearts in areas of leadership. Leaders serve the Lord by caring for, not dominating, the church. Jesus talked about this issue:

> But Jesus called them to Himself and said, "You know that the rulers of the Gentiles lord it over them, and those who are great exercise authority over them. Yet it shall not be so among you; but whoever desires to become great among you, let him be your servant."
> (Matthew 20:25–26)

# THE WITCHCRAFT OF REBELLION

> Has the LORD as great delight in burnt offerings and sacrifices, as in obeying the voice of the LORD? Behold, to obey is better than sacrifice, and to heed than the fat of rams. For rebellion is as the sin of witchcraft, and stubbornness is as iniquity and idolatry. Because you have rejected the word of the LORD, He also has rejected you from being king.
> (1 Samuel 15:22–23)

Saul was anointed to be king of Israel. He was given clear instructions to destroy the Amalekites, who were a great offense to God. But Saul disobeyed. He rebelled against God and saved some of the loot for himself and the people. Saul was afraid of the murmuring of the people; thus, he disregarded God's word. Although he retained a religious appearance, he was diverted from the worship of God and took some of the glory of the conquest for himself. Does the idea of taking glory that belongs to God sound familiar? Shortly thereafter, an evil spirit came upon Saul to torment him. (See 1 Samuel 16:14.)

There is an atmosphere of rebellion in our own time. Children rebel against parents; parents rebel against their employers; people rebel against the authority God has established over them in government; and government has rebelled against God by passing laws that permit all kinds of shameful and godless activities. Those who are openly homosexual dare God to condemn them. They demand equal rights and flout the laws of God. We have become a rebellious nation of individuals who think only of ourselves.

> WE HAVE SERVED AT A DIFFERENT ALTAR AND TURNED AWAY FROM GOD.

The witchcraft of rebellion in every form and flavor has overtaken our generation. Why are we surprised that children and teachers are shot down and killed when we have torn the laws of God off the walls of our schools? We permit "health organizations" to pass out condoms in public schools, giving tacit blessing to premarital sex among teens. We have served at a different altar and

43

turned away from God. Humanism reigns in government and public schools, and God has been asked to leave. The witchcraft of rebellion has infected our nation at every level. The result will be what it always has been: separation from God.

None of this is by coincidence. Witchcraft is part of a deliberate strategy to undermine our worship and fellowship with God.

# SATAN HAS A STRATEGY

Satan has a strategy. He isn't sitting around hell throwing darts at a dartboard to determine his next move. He knows exactly what he wants to do and to whom he wants to do it. *So should we.*

Satan's strategy is applied through three basic means: *intimidation, manipulation,* and *domination.* Satan tries to influence us and divert us from fellowship with God by scaring us, managing us, or overpowering us. His strategies are applied not only directly on us, but also through us. We try to intimidate or impress one another, manage what others think, or lift ourselves above them in pride. We must understand that there is an active plot against our families, the church, and every one of us individually. From the corporate CEO's office to the pastor's study, Satan employs his scheme through unwitting players. There are many "Simons" among us who are accepted and revered by many as community leaders and even representatives of God. The trappings are different, but domination and manipulative control are still the undercurrent.

# THIS IS WAR

This is war! And Satan's strategy is to wage war by using terrorism, psychological warfare, and overwhelming force. Many born-again believers are robbed and rendered ineffective because they are unaware of the devices that the enemy employs for their destruction. In the next chapters we will examine Satan's strategies of *intimidation, manipulation,* and *domination.*

# Chapter Three

---

# The Terrorist
# Tactic of
# Intimidation

# Chapter Three

---

# The Terrorist Tactic of Intimidation

*Then Caleb quieted the people before Moses, and said, "Let us go up at once and take possession, for we are well able to overcome it." But the men who had gone up with him said, "We are not able to go up against the people, for they are stronger than we." And they gave the children of Israel a bad report of the land which they had spied out, saying, "The land through which we have gone as spies is a land that devours its inhabitants, and all the people whom we saw in it are men of great stature. There we saw the giants (the descendants of Anak came from the giants);*

*and we were like grasshoppers in our own sight, and
so we were in their sight.*
—Numbers 13:30–33

# FEAR

We see the following kinds of stories all too often. A man straps explosives to himself and detonates them on a bus, killing himself and many others. Who will ever forget the bombing in Oklahoma City, when hundreds were killed by a truckload of volatile chemicals parked in front of a government building? Then there were those men who blew up a 747 over the skies of Scotland, killing men, women, and children of all ages and nationalities. Most recently, the World Trade Center towers and the Pentagon were attacked, causing many deaths and the destruction of the towers. Though the methods used and the causes served may have differed, all of these acts were acts of "terrorism."

Those who commit these heinous acts are called terrorists. A terrorist is essentially a coward serving a lost cause. They do not have the power or ability to win an outright confrontation, so they resort to terrorism to prove a point and get some attention.

Their chief objective is to put terror and fear into us. The terrorist believes that if he can scare us, he can *defeat* us, *distract* us, and *deny* us. Terrorism is a way in which an enemy of inferior strength can control a vastly superior foe. Terror is the single strongest weapon that any opposing force can employ because it can defeat us before we fire a shot. Terror is the weapon of intimidation.

We must differentiate here between fear and terrorism. Fear itself is a natural response to a threat. We would be foolish not to have some fear and respect for danger, whether it be natural or man-made. But to be controlled by fear, when fear is used as a deliberate tool of the enemy, is a different matter entirely. There is a major difference between healthy fear and terrorism.

## FEAR IN THE FAMILY

If you grow up in a family of five or six, one of your brothers or sisters inevitably becomes the thinker of the family pack—usually the eldest. This sibling sometimes gets the other children to do what he wants through fear. He may cause them to be afraid with his physical size, or perhaps he makes them afraid by causing them to feel stupid. This child controls the other children with terror. Of course, this is mostly learned behavior. He intimidates because someone or something else has intimidated him, whether it be parents or circumstances.

> **FEAR ITSELF IS A NATURAL RESPONSE TO A THREAT.**

This terrorism goes on in many families, including the family of God. Preachers can intimidate the people of God from the pulpit by preaching the judgment of God without the grace of God. These leaders betray their position as the under-shepherds of God's flock. I have seen

51

Christian leaders whose followers cower in fear when they walk into the room. They are shepherds who hold clubs over the heads of the sheep. In this way, the enemy uses fear to make God's flock afraid of their heavenly Father. Pastors and other leaders in the church must not lead by intimidation. Shepherds are to feed, guide, and protect the flock of God. The apostle Peter, who was asked by Jesus to care for the flock of God (John 21:15–17), gave instructions to other Christian leaders regarding the attitude of those who would shepherd God's flock:

> *The elders who are among you I exhort, I who am a fellow elder and a witness of the sufferings of Christ, and also a partaker of the glory that will be revealed: shepherd the flock of God which is among you, serving as overseers, not by compulsion but willingly, not for dishonest gain but eagerly; nor as being lords over those entrusted to you, but being examples to the flock; and when the Chief Shepherd appears, you will receive the crown of glory that does not fade away.*
>
> (1 Peter 5:1–4)

# FEAR AS A TOOL OF INFLUENCE

Fear is a powerful tool of influence. Satan's strategy is to make us afraid, thus preventing us from possessing the promises of God. When he makes us afraid, we take our eyes off God and focus on the object of fear the devil presents to us. Obstacles, threats, and circumstances overwhelm us. If he can distract us, we will take our eyes off God and His promises. Then Satan can effectively defeat us before we set one foot into our Promised Land.

Once defeated, even born-again believers can become depressed and open to further demonic oppression that keeps them ineffective in the kingdom of God.

The enemy can cause fear to control us by various means. We can have a fear of rejection, a fear of failure, a fear of success, a fear of responsibility, a fear of loneliness, even a fear of fear itself. Whatever the guise, fear will keep us on the wrong side of the river if we allow it to.

This was the case of Israel when God led them to the front porch of the Promised Land. The faithless majority of the spies saw the obstacles and took their eyes off God, focusing instead on giants and grasshoppers. They looked at their own ability, saying, *"We are not able"* (Numbers 13:31). They were right. They were not able in their own strength to overcome the inhabitants of the land. So they saw God's abundance as a devouring beast before which they were helpless.

Whenever we are poised to enter some new and greater dimension of God, the enemy will use fear to stop us in our tracks. It was fear that prevented Israel from entering into the land of promise. We must remember, though, that fear takes many, and sometimes less obvious, forms.

We've already mentioned a few. There is the fear of rejection, the fear of loneliness, the fear of failure, the fear of embarrassment, and the list goes on. All these prevent us from effectively employing our gifts in the body of Christ. The enemy sees the power and purpose that God is bringing us into, so he plants a minefield of fear on the frontier of our inheritance.

Even the most seasoned Christian can be a victim of intimidation. It seems that the greater the anointing, the greater the enemy's effort to terrorize us and bring us to a halt. I think of the great prophet Elijah, who, after slaying hundreds of false prophets and calling down the fire of God, was threatened by an evil queen named Jezebel.

> *And Ahab told Jezebel all that Elijah had done, also how he had executed all the prophets with the sword. Then Jezebel sent a messenger to Elijah, saying, "So let the gods do to me, and more also, if I do not make your life as the life of one of them by tomorrow about this time." And when he **saw** that, he arose and ran for his life, and went to Beersheba, which belongs to Judah, and left his servant there.* (1 Kings 19:1–3, emphasis added)

First Kings 19:3 tells us that when this great man of God *"saw"* this threat from Jezebel, he ran into the desert. He took

**GOD KNOWS THE ENEMY'S TACTICS.**

his eyes off the purpose and calling of God and he *"saw"* only fear. Later, God revealed Himself to Elijah in a powerful way, enabling him to continue in God's purpose.

God knows the enemy's tactics as well. Whenever God was about to do something great in the Bible, He prehandled the issue of fear.

Consider Moses and Israel on the western shores of the Red Sea. The Egyptians were behind them and the sea in front of them. That would be enough to make anyone afraid.

*Then they said to Moses, "Because there were no graves in Egypt, have you taken us away to die in the wilderness? Why have you so dealt with us, to bring us up out of Egypt? Is this not the word that we told you in Egypt, saying, 'Let us alone that we may serve the Egyptians?' For it would have been better for us to serve the Egyptians than that we should die in the wilderness." And Moses said to the people, "Do not be afraid. Stand still, and see the salvation of the LORD, which He will accomplish for you today. For the Egyptians whom you see today, you shall see again no more forever. The LORD will fight for you, and you shall hold your peace."* (Exodus 14:11–14)

When fear comes, it causes us to turn away from promise and back to bondage. The Israelites said, *"Let us alone."* Fear made them recoil; it paralyzed them. But into this fear God spoke through Moses, saying, *"Do not be afraid. Stand still, and see the salvation of the LORD."* In other words, "Take your eyes off the Egyptians and see what I will do." How many times have we turned our backs on God's salvation and looked at the problem instead of at the Lord?

In most instances in the Bible, when God was about to do something great, He dealt with fear and put His servants at peace.

• Think of God's words to Israel and Joshua as they entered to conquer the Promised Land.

*Have I not commanded you? Be strong and of good courage; **do not be afraid**, nor be dismayed, for*

*the* LORD *your God is with you wherever you go.*
(Joshua 1:9, emphasis added)

• Think of Jehoshaphat and Judah as they were about to enter into a battle with the enemies of God.

*And he said, "Listen, all you of Judah and you inhabitants of Jerusalem, and you, King Jehoshaphat! Thus says the* LORD *to you:* **'Do not be afraid** *nor dismayed because of this great multitude, for the battle is not yours, but God's.'"*
(2 Chronicles 20:15, emphasis added)

• Think of the people of Jerusalem rebuilding the walls and gates under Nehemiah.

*And I looked, and arose and said to the nobles, to the leaders, and to the rest of the people,* **"Do not be afraid** *of them. Remember the Lord, great and awesome, and fight for your brethren, your sons, your daughters, your wives, and your houses."*
(Nehemiah 4:14, emphasis added)

• Think of Mary as she was about to conceive Jesus by the Holy Spirit. This was the greatest deliverance of all.

*Then the angel said to her,* **"Do not be afraid***, Mary, for you have found favor with God. And behold, you will conceive in your womb and bring forth a Son, and shall call His name* JESUS.*"*
(Luke 1:30–31, emphasis added)

In the Bible, God tells us, in one form or another, 365 times not to be afraid. If we focus on fear, then we will be controlled by it. But if we really understand fear and how the enemy uses it, we can *turn the tables on terrorism.*

## TURNING THE TABLES ON TERRORISM

As I said before, terrorism is the weapon of a defeated foe. It will be thrown at us from every angle and every source. Whether it comes from inside or outside the church, fear will *distract* us, *deny* us, and *defeat* us if we allow it to do so. But God makes a promise to those who look to Him rather than at fear. His promise is to turn the tables on the enemy and make him *run*!

> TERRORISM IS THE WEAPON OF A DEFEATED FOE.

> *I will send My fear before you, I will cause confusion among all the people to whom you come, and will make all your enemies turn their backs to you.*
> (Exodus 23:27)

How do we turn the tables on the weapon of terrorism? How do we fight the fear that keeps us from God's best?

## FIGHTING FEAR WITH FOCUS

The best defense against fear is never to take our eyes off Jesus. In dealing with fear, it is important to focus on God's purpose rather than be distracted by the terrorism of the enemy. God's supreme purpose is to save mankind, and *you* are His strategy. The devil knows this all too well, so he will throw terror in front of you to scare you out of fulfilling God's purpose.

Every time a soul is saved, a major battle has been won. Think about it for a moment. What is it that prevents us from sharing our testimony or the Gospel with a friend or a neighbor? *Fear!* We are afraid that we might be embarrassed or that we will be rejected in some way, so we clam up and watch our friend struggle and slide into hell. If we fail to share the Good News because of the terror tactics of the enemy, then we have allowed him to win.

We don't serve a God who is standing over in the corner scratching His head, trying to figure out how He will bring us out of our latest dilemma. He delivered us before He brought us into the problem. He brought us to the threshold of promise and continuous victory. But we must wake up to His deliverance. The battle has already been won! We need only to appropriate it.

> *You will keep him in perfect peace, whose mind is stayed* [focused] *on You, because he trusts in You. Trust in the LORD forever, for in YAH, the LORD, is everlasting strength.* (Isaiah 26:3–4)

# FIGHTING FEAR WITH FELLOWSHIP

Another antidote for the poison of fear is fellowship. The purpose of fellowship is to encourage each other, to handle the fears we each bring to the body. We come together as a body in order to *remind* one another about God. We come together to *minister* encouragement to each other. We come together to *learn* more of God and gain confidence in Him. We come together to *tell* stories of God's victory over the enemy's terror tactics.

Hear the Word of God:

*Now I myself am confident concerning you, my brethren, that you also are full of goodness, filled with all knowledge, able also to admonish one another.*        (Romans 15:14)

and,

*Let the peace of God rule in your hearts, to which also you were called in one body; and be thankful. Let the word of Christ dwell in you richly in all wisdom, teaching and admonishing one another in psalms and hymns and spiritual songs, singing with grace in your hearts to the Lord.*        (Colossians 3:15–16)

and,

*Now we exhort you, brethren, warn those who are unruly, comfort the fainthearted* [those who are being terrorized]*, uphold the weak, be patient with all.*        (1 Thessalonians 5:14)

and,

*Therefore strengthen the hands which hang down, and the feeble knees, and make straight paths for your feet,*

*so that what is lame may not be dislocated, but rather
be healed.* (Hebrews 12:12–13)

# FIGHTING FEAR WITH FACTS

It is important to any military campaign that those
on the front lines have all the facts about the enemy. An
intelligence-gathering operation must take place in order
to understand the position and strength of the enemy in
relation to ours. The enemy always employs fear because
he cannot win. Perhaps we can learn something here.
When we are the most afraid, the devil is even more
afraid of us. You see, whatever fight we are in, wherever
God has led us, the fight belongs to God, not to us. When
we read the Bible and memorize Scriptures, we are ingest-
ing an antidote for fear. When the enemy throws his terrorist tactics before us, we must not listen to him but listen
to what God says instead. And what does God tell us
about the battles we fight?

> *And he shall say to them, "Hear, O Israel: Today you
> are on the verge of battle with your enemies. Do not let
> your heart faint, do not be afraid, and do not tremble
> or be terrified because of them; for the LORD your God
> is He who goes with you, to fight for you against your
> enemies, to save you."* (Deuteronomy 20:3–4)

and,

> *You will chase your enemies, and they shall fall by
> the sword before you. Five of you shall chase a hun-
> dred, and a hundred of you shall put ten thousand to*

*flight; your enemies shall fall by the sword before you.*
(Leviticus 26:7–8)

And, in Jesus' own words,

*These things I have spoken to you, that in Me you may have peace. In the world you will have tribulation; but be of good cheer* [don't be afraid], *I have overcome the world.* (John 16:33)

When I am faced with fear, I remember that I need to get my priorities in order. The best way to drown out the word of fear is with the sounds of praise. In 2 Chronicles, Jerusalem was faced with strong enemies who wanted to ransack the city. Instead of gathering swords and spears and measuring the might of the army, King Jehoshaphat held a praise festival.

*And Jehoshaphat feared, and set himself to seek the LORD, and proclaimed a fast throughout all Judah. So Judah gathered together to ask help from the LORD; and from all the cities of Judah they came to seek the LORD....Then the Spirit of the LORD came upon Jahaziel the son of Zechariah, the son of Benaiah, the son of Jeiel, the son of Mattaniah, a Levite of the sons of Asaph, in the midst of the assembly. And he said, "Listen, all you of Judah and you inhabitants of Jerusalem, and you, King Jehoshaphat! Thus says the LORD to you: 'Do not be afraid nor dismayed because of this great multitude, for the battle is not yours, but God's....You will not need to fight in this*

*battle. Position yourselves, stand still and see the sal-*
*vation of the LORD, who is with you, O Judah and*
*Jerusalem!' Do not fear or be dismayed; tomorrow go*
*out against them, for the LORD is with you."...And*
*when he had consulted with the people, he appointed*
*those who should sing to the LORD, and who should*
*praise the beauty of holiness, as they went out before*
*the army and were saying: "Praise the LORD, for His*
*mercy endures forever." Now when they began to*
*sing and to praise, the LORD set ambushes against*
*the people of Ammon, Moab, and Mount Seir,*
*who had come against Judah; and they were defeated.*
(2 Chronicles 20:3–4, 14–15, 17, 21–22)

Perhaps the real key to spiritual warfare is to remember who is fighting the battle. The people did not shout at the enemy or bind evil sprits; they lifted up the name of the Lord, and the Lord set the ambush for the enemy.

THE KEY IS TO REMEMBER WHO IS FIGHTING THE BATTLE.

Satan is focused on distracting us with fear. We must learn to recognize his plan and let God into the fight. We may be in the battle, but the battle belongs to God. God hasn't left us alone to fight Satan. Without these facts, we will lose hope, and the host of hell will keep us ineffective. Begin the process of discovery by taking the Word of God into your heart. God's Holy Word is the weapon of truth and knowledge.

When the enemy threatens us with terror, we must fight with the facts—and the main fact is that the battle belongs to the Lord.

# THE FINAL WORD ON FEAR

Remember that we began this chapter with a story of defeat and distraction at the frontier of promise. We need to have the same attitude and understanding that Joshua and Caleb did if we are to defeat the enemy's terrorism. Listen:

> But Joshua the son of Nun and Caleb the son of Jephunneh, who were among those who had spied out the land, tore their clothes; and they spoke to all the congregation of the children of Israel, saying: "The land we passed through to spy out is **an exceedingly good land**. If the LORD delights in us, then **He will bring us** into this land and give it to us, 'a land which flows with milk and honey.' Only do not rebel against the LORD, nor fear the people of the land, **for they are our bread**; their protection has departed from them, and the LORD is with us. **Do not fear them**."
>
> (Numbers 14:6–9, emphasis added)

Joshua and Caleb understood a few things that you and I need to remember as we turn the tables on terrorism. They summarize what we have been saying in this chapter.

- When the enemy is using fear, God is bringing us into *"an exceedingly good land."*

- We don't fight in our own strength. *"He will bring us."*

- The enemy is a defeated and desperate foe. *"They are our bread."*

- God alone is worthy of fear. *"Do not fear them."*

If there is anything that we can be sure of, it is that we will face the terrorism of the enemy as we move on in God. But we cannot be controlled by the terror of the enemy when we know the truth of God.

> *For God has not given us a spirit of fear, but of power and of love and of a sound mind.*    (2 Timothy 1:7)

# Chapter Four

# Manipulation: The Psychological Warfare of the Enemy

# Chapter Four

# Manipulation: The Psychological Warfare of the Enemy

In the 1930s and '40s, Hitler was able to convince an entire nation that people of a particular ethnicity were inferior and should be eliminated. Of course, the Jewish people were the most frequently targeted group. The Germans instituted a program of "disinformation," which is to say, they deliberately put out the wrong facts to the German people. This was done in every phase of life, from the media, to art, to the classroom. Jews were seen as subhuman and not worthy of the air they breathed. This manipulation of the truth was so effective that by the time Hitler implemented the "Final Solution," those who murdered Jewish children thought they were doing the right thing.

In a similar vein, widespread racism in the United States resulted in the devaluation of African-Americans. Black and white children grew up believing that black children were somehow inferior. In fact, I recall reading about a particular study where little black girls were given a choice of either black or white dolls, and they chose the white ones as the more desirable. Whether we call it the "Final Solution" or "segregation" or "apartheid," the strategy and inspiration are motivated by Satan.

## MANIPULATION IS ONE OF SATAN'S MOST EFFECTIVE WEAPONS.

One of Satan's most effective weapons in distracting and influencing us is *manipulation*. To manipulate means to manage people or circumstances to gain an advantage. What is being manipulated is the mind through the offering of lies and half-truths. There is a deliberate attempt to manage what people think. When nations go to war, they frequently employ tactics that seek to manipulate what the opposition thinks. This is called "psychological warfare." Satan, our enemy, also engages in a kind of manipulation in which he employs his own tactics of psychological warfare.

# TACTICS OF PSYCHOLOGICAL WARFARE

Psychological warfare includes the manipulation of facts to discredit what is true. The basic idea is to create doubt in the minds of the enemy. In Paul's second epistle to the Corinthians, there is a picture of the tactics that Satan uses to distract us from God and His truth.

> *For though we walk in the flesh, we do not war according to the flesh. For the weapons of our warfare are not carnal but mighty in God for pulling down strongholds, casting down* **arguments** *and* **every high thing** *that exalts itself against the knowledge of God, bringing every thought into captivity to the obedience of Christ, and being ready to punish all disobedience when your obedience is fulfilled.*
> (2 Corinthians 10:3–6, emphasis added)

The apostle Paul preached the Gospel of grace to the Gentiles. But there were those who opposed his message. When Paul planted churches in the area of Corinth, Judaizers came from Jerusalem to preach a fleshly and legalistic kind of Christianity. They taught that the converted Gentiles should follow the Jewish Law, including circumcision and dietary regulations. The way that the Judaizers chose to wage war against Paul's Gospel was to call into question his motives and his authority. If they could not defeat the message, then they would discredit the messenger. They accused Paul of hypocrisy, saying that he spoke one way through letters and another in person. They did not like what he preached or the manner in which it was presented. (See 2 Corinthians 10:1–2.)

The gospel that the Judaizers preached raised up high walls between man and God. It sought to keep man in control of his salvation and his relationship with God. Does this sound familiar? *"You will be like God"* (Genesis 3:5). The result was that Paul, in return, waged war against those things that were raised up *"against the knowledge of God."*

What exactly was Paul warring against? He was warring against *arguments, actions,* and *attitudes* that separate people from God. He referred to them as *"strongholds,"* a place of enemy control. Paul warred against a legalistic and manipulative kind of gospel that kept its hearers in bondage and separated from God.

Remember, Satan's objective is to divert and distract us from fellowship with God. The battleground of this psychological warfare is the mind. Whereas Satan's tactics of *intimidation* seek to divert us from God by fear, his tactic of *manipulation* seeks to create doubts and distractions to preoccupy our minds, thus preventing us from fellowshipping with God. The tactics of manipulation take place in every area of our lives, from the boardroom to the bedroom, but they are most destructive in the body of Christ. This demonic psychological warfare takes place among brothers and sisters in the body of Christ by several means. The first is what the Bible calls *"arguments"* (2 Corinthians 10:5).

# ARGUMENTS

An argument in the biblical sense is a reasoning, an opinion, or perhaps a word. These arguments are expressed in a variety of ways, including criticism, gossip, innuendo, sarcasm, moodiness, and religious pretense, as well as others. Satan rides into our churches on the critical opinions we voice about someone or something. He launches his attack through the angry and manipulative words issued from a carnal heart.

Over the years, I have seen these kinds of arguments in the church. You see, when we come to Christ, our spirits are saved, but our minds are still in the ghetto. When we don't renew our minds according to the Word of God, they stay carnal. Some of those carnal tendencies sit in the pews of our churches. When individuals don't get their way, they begin to criticize the preacher or others in leadership. They voice their "concern" about the issues they wish to manipulate to their favor. The world calls this "pressure"; the sanctified call it "concern." What was "gossip" in the world becomes a "conversation of concern" in the church. The result and the sources are the same, whether it is inside or outside the body of Christ. They are demonic!

> SATAN RIDES INTO OUR CHURCHES ON OUR COMPLAINTS AND CRITICISM.

It is amazing how a single sentence motivated by iniquity can ruin an otherwise great day. Perhaps you have experienced something like the following situation.

You get up on Sunday morning and start getting ready to go to church. There is the hum of a hymn breaking the Sabbath air, and you are feeling great! To your surprise and delight, the kids are ready on time, and everything is going smoothly. This is going to be *your* day. You jump into the car and pop a worship tape into the tape deck. You are happy and excited and worshiping God on the way to church. You are on time for the first time in a year. You look great, your spouse looks great, and your kids are the very picture of the Christian upbringing you have provided. Everything is "perfect." As you pull into the church parking lot, you see that the best parking spot is open, and you pull right in. Now, serene, you walk into the church with your head lifted up worshipfully in the clouds. But the minute you get inside the door, there's somebody with whom you had an earlier disagreement blocking the path to your seat.

"Oh, I know you aren't going to just walk by me and not speak," the person says in a rather condescending tone.

Suddenly, all of what you felt is gone. Anger and contempt have replaced your peace and power. Your head drops down from the clouds and begins to throb with stress. Where only moments ago all was "perfect" and you were ready to ascend to heaven with praise, now you are a defeated lump of flesh.

What happened to you? An argument or word from another person—inspired and produced by iniquity—just reached out and touched you. Suddenly, all the warm worshipful thoughts you had about the Lord are drowned out by the sound of your own heart pounding out a rising blood pressure level. You have been derailed, diverted, and distracted from fellowship with God. You have been the victim of an argument of Satan's psychological warfare. He has manipulated and managed your mind to distract you from God. And it worked. You couldn't worship after that even if you had angels on either arm singing into your injured ears.

The substance of what that person said to you at the back door is not the issue. Any number of arguments produces the same kinds of responses. We can get sidetracked by doctrinal disputes regarding how many angels can stand on the head of a pin, or where we should place the new piano in the sanctuary. From the color of the carpet to the mode of communion, Satan can argue us out of fellowship with God.

Perhaps the most frequent targets of our words of doubt and criticism are the pastors and other leaders in the church. There are those carnal minds that feel their "gifts" are not being used to the fullest, or perhaps their voices are not being heard and their opinions are not given the weight they deserve. Thus they begin an assault against those who lead them by whispering "concerns" expressed in terms of great passion and love of God. All the while they attack God's ordained leadership and draw other like-minded people to themselves. A demonic strategy has been employed through them, which sometimes results in church division or even a church split.

Sometimes there are legitimate reasons for concern regarding church leaders, but these are never to be processed among brothers and sisters. These problems must first be taken directly to the leader in question. As soon as we voice "concern" to a peer in the congregation, we have invited the devil into the church. Note that in the Corinthian church, the very ones who attacked Paul for speaking with two different tones never approached him directly. Instead, they allowed themselves to become tools of the enemy to separate people from God and one another.

The enemy can control us not only by what we *say*, but also by what we *do*—through our actions.

# ACTIONS

How many times have you seen people stay away from fellowship with the church body because they were offended in some way? They believe that by withholding themselves from others, they somehow control them. It is not unlike what my brother used to do with his manipulative tantrums. They use our love as a weapon against us. (They do not realize that they have played right into the plan of the enemy; they are separated and isolated from other believers and the Lord.) Though they may not admit it, this isolation is a way to manipulate others in the body into agreeing with them against the one who offended them. Perhaps this is why people hop from church to church, leaving a trail of injured people in their wakes. The writer of Hebrews instructed us,

> PEOPLE SOMETIMES USE OUR LOVE AS A WEAPON AGAINST US.

*And let us consider one another in order to stir up love and good works, not forsaking the assembling of ourselves together, as is the manner of some, but exhorting one another, and so much the more as you see the Day approaching.* (Hebrews 10:24–25)

There are actions of commission and omission that some employ to manage the minds of others. They seek to manage or influence other people's minds by what they do or don't do. It is probably those things that they don't do that are the most effective in their manipulation. For example, some people withhold love; others withhold their tithes and offerings.

Money should never become a weapon. Withholding your tithe invites a curse. It opens a demonic doorway into the area of your finances.

*"Will a man rob God? Yet you have robbed Me! But you say, 'In what way have we robbed You?' In tithes and offerings. **You are cursed with a curse**, for you have robbed Me, even this whole nation. Bring all the tithes into the storehouse, that there may be food in My house, and try Me now in this," says the LORD of hosts, "If I will not open for you the windows of heaven and pour out for you such blessing that there will not be room enough to receive it."* (Malachi 3:8–10, emphasis added)

Money does not belong to the one who holds it. It belongs to God. In one sense, when we withhold money from the church, we are trying to manipulate God. God will not be managed!

Any action that we take with the motive of influencing the behavior of someone else, plays into the hands of Satan. And the more we play the game, the more of a foothold he gains. We become centers of his influence.

What we say and what we do can be used by the enemy for the purposes of diverting us from God. But there is another factor, and that is the stronghold of pride. All of us live behind this stronghold to some extent. It concerns the *attitude* with which we say or do something.

# ATTITUDES

The king of Tyre is a biblical type of Satan. All of his iniquity and arrogance stemmed from pride.

> *Son of man, say to the prince of Tyre, "Thus says the Lord GOD: 'Because your heart is lifted up, and you say, "I am a god, I sit in the seat of gods, in the midst of the seas," yet you are a man, and not a god, though you set your heart as the heart of a god.'"* (Ezekiel 28:2)

As we described in Chapter One, Satan caught a glimpse of himself and became proud. He is the originator of pride, and he imparted iniquity to us through the fall of Adam and Eve. Again, it's the old lie that we can *"be like God"* (Genesis 3:5). We begin to see ourselves as being above others.

Pride is an exalted opinion of ourselves. Pride places us on a judgment bench from which we look down on other people. We hold "lesser" people and opinions in contempt. We may not be openly hostile to those we judge, but we talk down to them. We treat them as children and give them no respect. We issue our judicial opinions about their value. If there is one common indicator as to whether or not we are prideful, it is how we value other people. If we see others as inferior to us, then pride has done its work. The result is separation and persecution of those we value less.

**PRIDE IS INDICATED BY HOW WE VALUE OTHER PEOPLE.**

God warns us about pride throughout the Bible.

*Do not lift up your horn on high; do not speak with a stiff neck.* (Psalm 75:5)

and,

*Pride goes before destruction, and a haughty spirit before a fall. Better to be of a humble spirit with the lowly, than to divide the spoil with the proud.* (Proverbs 16:18–19)

Judgment is God's business. We are not in any position to question Him or devalue other people. The problem with pride is that, like other forms of manipulation, it invites judgment.

*For exaltation comes neither from the east nor from the west nor from the south. But God is the Judge: He puts down one, and exalts another. For in the hand of the LORD there is a cup, and the wine is red; it is fully mixed, and He pours it out; surely its dregs*

*shall all the wicked of the earth drain and drink down.*
(Psalm 75:6–8)

and,

*A man's pride will bring him low, but the humble in spirit will retain honor.* (Proverbs 29:23)

Jesus instructed us not to judge others because we would invite the same judgment upon ourselves (Matthew 7:1). We are to release others to the judgment of God. Whether through criticism or condescension, pride is the main flavor of iniquity. We must examine not only our words and actions, but also the attitudes with which each are generated.

# TEARING DOWN STRONGHOLDS

The first step in our demolition of enemy strongholds is to realize that we all have them. Yes, even believers filled with the Holy Spirit can come under demonic influence.

One time I was in the middle of ministering against satanic curses when I realized that there was a stronghold in my own life in the area of criticism. Before then, I had believed that Christians, saved and filled with the Holy Spirit, could not be oppressed by demons. How could a blood-bought Christian be part of the plan and program of Satan in the earth? I truly believed that a fountain couldn't bring forth both bitter and sweet water.

And that is absolutely true; a fountain cannot bring forth bitter and sweet water. But a human being can most definitely speak well in one sentence and absolute evil in the next. We see this truth demonstrated through Peter, who was used by the Holy Spirit to reveal Jesus as the Messiah, only to be rebuked by the Messiah a short time later because of Satan's working through him! (See Matthew 16:16, 21–23.)

What I learned was that strongholds are in the mind, not the spirit, of a believer. When we come to Christ, we are His; however, our minds have not caught up to our spirits. There is a war being waged in our minds to see who will control it, God or flesh and the devil. Paul spoke of this same thing:

> For we know that the law is spiritual, but I am carnal, sold under sin. For what I am doing, I do not understand. For what I will to do, that I do not practice; but what I hate, that I do. If, then, I do what I will not to do, I agree with the law that it is good. But now, it is no longer I who do it, but sin that dwells in me. For I know that in me (that is, in my flesh) nothing good dwells; for to will is present with me, but how to perform what is good I do not find. For the good that I will to do, I do not do; but the evil I will not to do, that I practice. Now if I do what I will not to do, it is no longer I who do it, but sin that dwells in me. I find then a law, that evil is present with me, the one who wills to do good.
> (Romans 7:14–21)

It is clear that Paul understood that though he belonged to God, there was still a war going on in him, seeking to distract him from the Lord. Although we must realize that there is a war going on in us, we also must realize that God alone will win that war. Think of Joshua as he commanded Israel to march around the walls of Jericho. The walls did not fall because of Israel's military might, but because they walked out the word of the Lord to them.

We cannot win by our own ability. As Paul said,

*O wretched man that I am! Who will deliver me from this body of death? I thank God; through Jesus Christ our Lord! So then, with the mind I myself serve the law of God, but with the flesh the law of sin.*
(Romans 7:24–25)

We can tear down the strongholds of *arguments*, *actions*, and *attitudes* through which the enemy manipulates us by doing what Paul instructed the Corinthians to do. We must *"bring every thought into captivity to the obedience of Christ"* (2 Corinthians 10:5). In other words, we must say what Jesus would say and do what Jesus would do—all with the same attitude of humility He had. Humility is not groveling; it is knowing who we are in Christ Jesus.

> HUMILITY IS KNOWING WHO WE ARE IN CHRIST.

The antidote for the disinformation that the devil uses to manipulate us is the truth of God's Word. We free ourselves from the enemy's psychological warfare of manipulation when we receive the truth and then walk in it. As we continue in the truth of God's Word, we will escape the devices of the enemy.

> Then Jesus said to those Jews who believed Him, "If you abide in My word, you are My disciples indeed. And you shall know the truth, and the truth shall make you free." (John 8:31–32)

# Chapter Five

---

# Domination: The Use of Overwhelming Force

# Chapter Five

# Domination: The Use of Overwhelming Force

Some time ago I was accorded the great privilege of speaking in a large and well-known church. I was honored by the invitation and excited at the prospect of speaking in this particular church. Imagine, George Bloomer, from the projects of Brooklyn, was coming to preach in the church of this well-known and influential pastor.

I was instructed by the pastor to arrive a little while after the service began so that I would not have to sit through all the preliminary announcements and such. When I arrived at the front entrance of this impressive facility, there was no one waiting to direct me. Walking in the front entrance, I felt awestruck. There were television cameras everywhere and the place was jam-packed. This was going to be so exciting!

My heart was filled with the prospects and possibilities of speaking from that renowned pulpit. I was rehearsing my sermon in my mind and thought it might be a good idea to go over my notes one last time. At the same time, my mind and attention were caught up in the background music and activity on the other side of the sanctuary doors. My heart was awhirl with the anticipation of this tremendous opportunity. In the midst of this impressive moment, I put my hand on the doorknob and pulled open the sanctuary door. The sound and excitement grew the farther I pulled it open.

Suddenly, I felt the jerk of someone rudely pulling the door out of my hand. I lost my grasp on the doorknob as it closed sharply before my stunned eyes and face. There I stood, outside the sanctuary, alone and deflated. My fervor was extinguished in a moment's time as if smothered by a wet blanket.

I said to myself, "Okay, maybe I shouldn't have touched the door. I'm in the wrong here." I had been in the church for a long time and should have known better than to just walk through a sanctuary door. After all, they could not have known it was I, the "Special Guest Preacher," on the other side of the door. But just as the swelling of my wounded ego was going down, insult was added to injury. The lady usher who had so rudely jerked the door out of my hand, dampening my excitement, slipped open the door and came back for more.

Focusing her widened eyes at me and wagging her head from side to side, she spoke *at* me in the most condescending of tones: *"You see this door? Do not put your hands on this door. Anytime you come to this church and you see this door closed, you just wait until I open it. They're up there praying; what's wrong with you?"* Then she again shut the door in my stunned face.

I was breathless! "Well, I know exactly what I'm preaching about tonight," I said to myself—"carnal church workers!" Now I would have my "pound of flesh"! She would be one sorry usher. How dare she insult me and treat me like some insignificant no-account nothing from the projects? I was the "Special Guest Preacher."

Just then, a young man came up and warmly greeted me. He said, "Come here with me." But I was so stunned and deflated by the lady usher that I could scarcely hear this man. I was out to get that "Jezebel." I was serious!

The young man, sent by the pastor to take care of my needs, took me down some steps and through a tunnel that came up into the pastor's office adjoining the platform. As I stood in the pastor's office, I gathered myself together. Then, after putting on my pastor's robe, I made a grand entrance onto the platform. As I strolled out onto the platform, the offending usher, with her condescending attitude, was standing at her door. When she saw me, she shriveled into the corner with her eyes turning downward so as not to catch my direct gaze. She had not realized with whom she had trifled. I was the "Preacher"—the honored guest speaker for the day. It was I who was to bring the Word of God. It was I who now stood in the holy majesty dressed in flowing ecclesiastical robes behind the pulpit. And now it was judgment day. She was toast!

How would I do it? What could I say to put her in her place? She was only an usher, while I was the preacher. Thoughts and strategies filled my mind as I sat there on the platform behind the pulpit. Then the praise broke out, and after a little while I was called up to minister. Suddenly, as I stood behind that renowned pulpit, the Holy Spirit took over. All the words set to spew forth from my wounded heart were now stuck in my throat. I wasn't able to "preach my thing" or "say my stuff." In an instant the Lord flooded me with His presence and brought me to His footstool. Without a word I was delivered of my arrogant and vengeful thinking. The Holy Spirit arrested me with His glory before I could say a word. By God's grace alone, I was able to minister.

> WE ALL STAND EQUALLY IN THE GRACE OF JESUS.

As the Lord continued to cleanse me, I glanced at the usher. It was like looking in a spiritual mirror. I had wanted to use my position to crush and destroy this usher. I had wanted to use my holy appearance to crush tears of repentance out of her. But then the Lord changed that.

Though I didn't feel delivered from my animosity completely, I realized that I had been thinking pretty highly of myself. At that moment, I realized, as Paul said, that we all stood equally in the grace of God of Jesus Christ.

> *For I say, through the grace given to me, to everyone who is among you, not to think of himself more highly than he ought to think, but to think soberly, as God has dealt to each one a measure of faith.* (Romans 12:3)

What happened there? Satan used an emotional bruise to start a war. This was part of his deliberate strategy to wound and kill another brother or sister in the Lord. Although we both should have been focusing on God, we were ambushed by pride and diverted by conflict. That is always Satan's strategy, his never-ending theme: distraction, diversion, and disharmony with God and one another. Without the intervention of the Holy Spirit and His gentle conviction, the day would have been lost.

So I ministered to the congregation (not on carnal church workers), finished up, and was going about my post-service business when this woman approached me to apologize. My heart now calmed, I was ready to hear her apology.

"I'm so sorry for the way I treated you," she said.

As she began to speak, I felt badly. But then she added, "If I had known you were the preacher, I would have never spoken to you like that."

When she said that, I realized that her apology was political, and my flesh rose up once again. After my first encounter with her, I had asked myself, "How dare she speak to me in such a manner?" I asked myself a lot in that short question. It was a clear indicator that I had placed myself above this sister somehow. When a preacher thinks that way, he is more likely serve the sheep up on a platter than serve the sheep in the love of Christ. By the wonderful grace of God, I had repented of my self-exaltation and now extended mercy to this sister.

Nevertheless, her second qualifying remark caused me to wonder how many came through that door on a weekly basis who probably didn't return to the church again because of her nasty, condescending attitude. Then again, I wondered how many times I had spoken down to people from my own pulpit. The same shoe fit both of us. Indeed, it fits most of us.

# OVERWHELMING FORCE

When Satan can't scare us by terrorism or manage us with psychological warfare, he tries to crush us through the overwhelming force of domination. This is the tactic that an army uses to utterly destroy their opponent. It is a "blitzkrieg" strategy that simply overpowers an enemy through brute force. As with the other strategies of distraction, we become tools in Satan's hand to crush and dominate others, keeping them from the grace of God.

This was the strategy that Satan employed in the events at the church where I was the guest speaker. Ironically, both the usher and myself were the channels through which Satan employed the strategy of overwhelming force. Each of us tried to put the other in our respective places while at the same time guarding our own. Both of us thought we were something and that the other was nothing. We were both wrong.

We were standing in a place set aside for the worship of God, and we could not get our minds off our own positions. Both of us tried to dominate the other, looking down from our lofty positions. Both of us were operating in the flesh. This same scene is played out with different characters in different settings every day and in many different arenas of life. We try to dominate one another in the workplace, in the family, and, most appallingly, in the church. Why? Because, though we are saved, there is still a part of us that is not submitted to God. We are living or walking in the flesh rather than in the spirit as spiritual people.

> WHEN WE TRY TO DOMINATE ONE ANOTHER, WE ARE OPERATING IN THE FLESH.

*I say then: Walk in the Spirit, and you shall not fulfill the lust of the flesh. For the flesh lusts against the Spirit, and the Spirit against the flesh; and these are contrary to one another, so that you do not do the things that you wish. But if you are led by the Spirit, you are not under the law.* (Galatians 5:16–18) and,

*For those who live according to the flesh set their minds on the things of the flesh, but those who live according to the Spirit, the things of the Spirit. For to be carnally minded is death, but to be spiritually minded is life and peace.* (Romans 8:5–6)

We could say this another way: "The flesh ignores the spirit." To live by the flesh is to live by the same things that motivated us before we were saved: *"the lust of the flesh, the lust of the eyes* [mind], *and the pride of life"* (1 John 2:16). Look at the progression: flesh, mind, and pride, of which the latter is the fuel for the use of overwhelming force.

All of these are associated with the three strategies Satan uses to distract us from God. *Intimidation* has to do with the flesh, *manipulation* with the mind, and *domination* with pride or self-exaltation. If we look carefully, we will see Satan's full array of strategies employed throughout the Bible, even in his dealings with Jesus Himself.

*So when the woman saw that the tree was good for food, that it was pleasant to the eyes, and a tree desirable to make one wise, she took of its fruit and ate.* (Genesis 3:6)

Do you see the enemy's arsenal? Look at this verse more closely:

• *"So when the woman saw that the tree was good for food."* This is the flesh.

- *"It was pleasant to the eyes."* Here's the mind.

- *"A tree desirable to make one wise."* This is pride.

We see the same strategies in the wilderness when the enemy tempted Jesus.

- *"The devil said to Him, 'If You are the Son of God, command this stone to become bread'"* (Luke 4:3). This appeals to the flesh.

- *"Then the devil, taking Him up on a high mountain, showed Him all the kingdoms of the world in a moment of time"* (verse 5). This appeals to the mind.

- *"Then he brought Him to Jerusalem, set Him on the pinnacle of the temple, and said to Him, 'If You are the Son of God, throw Yourself down from here'"* (verse 9). This appeals to pride of position.

> PRIDE IS THE RESULT OF THINKING THAT WE ARE MORE THAN WE ARE.

Pride is a result of thinking that we are more than we are. It is Satan's oldest weapon. Again, he tells us, "You can be like God." Part of us believes him. When we believe him, we use our position to dominate other people. We *"bite and devour one another,"* as Paul said in Galatians 5:15.

# OPPORTUNITIES FOR FORCE

Pride is an important issue because, in this strategy, we rob God of worship. Pride is, in effect, self-worship. If our eyes are on ourselves, then they will not be focused on the Lord. God cannot be seated on the thrones of our hearts if we are seated there ourselves. Satan does not always try to get us to worship him right away; sometimes he leads us to worship ourselves first, and we call that *pride*.

At no time does the strategy of overwhelming force have a greater opportunity than when we have been wounded in some way. When we are wounded, we remove our saintly suits and put on judge's robes. We feel that we have a right to judge the one who has wounded us, just as I did when the usher offended me. Our *flesh* is offended, our *mind* is distracted, and our *pride* takes over. "Here comes the judge!" But we are not carnal; we are spiritual creatures. When we are wounded, we are to restore in the Spirit rather than wound in the flesh.

> *My friends, if someone is caught in any kind of wrong-doing, those of you who are spiritual should set him right; but you must do it in a gentle way. And keep an eye on yourselves, so that you will not be tempted, too. Help carry one another's burdens, and in this way you will obey the law of Christ. If you think you are something when you are really nothing, you are only deceiving yourself.* (Galatians 6:1–3 GNT)

# POSITION

The dangers and opportunities to use overwhelming force lurk in the hearts of leaders in the church as well. Some leaders don't want to be held accountable.

Self-exalted people don't want to be disciplined. But all leaders are "under-shepherds" of the Good Shepherd, Jesus Christ. They are therefore accountable for their personal morals and attitudes toward the sheep, whom they are given the privilege of serving.

> *But Jesus called them to Himself and said to them, "You know that those who are considered rulers over the Gentiles lord it over them, and their great ones exercise authority over them. Yet it shall not be so among you; but whoever desires to become great among you shall be your servant. And whoever of you desires to be first shall be slave of all. For even the Son of Man did not come to be served, but to serve, and to give His life a ransom for many."* (Mark 10:42–45)

Anyone who knows anything should be able to discern that leadership and dictatorship are two different things, just as authority and domination are two different things. My example of this church visit could be replayed in the Sunday school department or anywhere else in the church where the people of God allow prideful thinking to direct their steps. Leaders in the church must remember that they are one of the sheep as well. They need to keep in mind that the flock belongs to God. The authority belongs to God. The worship and glory all belong to God. If we succumb to pride and self-exaltation, then we are on our own. The grace of God cannot flow to us or through us until we are submitted to Him. Grace always flows from the greater to the lesser.

*Yes, all of you be submissive to one another, and be clothed with humility, for "God resists the proud, but gives grace to the humble." Therefore humble yourselves under the mighty hand of God, that He may exalt you in due time, casting all your care upon Him, for He cares for you.*                    (1 Peter 5:5–7)

# HOW IS YOUR WALK?

How do we determine the character of our walk? Are we walking with people or over them? Are we walking in such a way that demonstrates the lordship of Christ in our lives? You and I must walk (live) in such a way so as to keep our eyes on God. We must walk by the Spirit, walk in love, and walk in humility.

# WALK BY THE SPIRIT

*I say then: Walk in the Spirit, and you shall not fulfill the lust of the flesh.*                    (Galatians 5:16)

When we are walking by the Spirit, we are living with eyes lifted toward heaven. We are walking as Jesus did, which means we make pleasing the Father our priority. We do not walk independently, but we take each step in the footprints of God's leading.

*Most assuredly, I say to you, the Son can do nothing of Himself, but what He sees the Father do; for whatever He does, the Son also does in like manner....I can of*

*Myself do nothing. As I hear, I judge; and My judgment is righteous, because I do not seek My own will but the will of the Father who sent Me.*     (John 5:19, 30)

When we live by the Spirit, we live in a way that pleases God. We are no longer concerned with our own plans and our own image. Walking by the Spirit is a moment-by-moment decision to believe God. Our old iniquitous nature is gone; it has been buried with Christ. We are no longer subject to fear or manipulation. *"We were buried with Him through baptism into death, that just as Christ was raised from the dead by the glory of the Father, even so we also should walk in newness of life"* (Romans 6:4).

We must also walk in love.

# WALK IN LOVE

*Then one of them, a lawyer, asked Him a question, testing Him, and saying, "Teacher, which is the great commandment in the law?" Jesus said to him, "'You shall love the LORD your God with all your heart, with all your soul, and with all your mind.' This is the first and great commandment. And the second is like it: 'You shall love your neighbor as yourself.' On these two commandments hang all the Law and the Prophets."*     (Matthew 22:35–40)

Love is the greatest law and governing principle of the kingdom of God. James called it *"the royal law"* in James 2:8. But, because it is everything opposite to the carnal nature of the old man, it must be contended for. God's kind of love is not a mere emotion; it is a conscious decision. We can set out each day determined to love regardless of the events and people we encounter. We can be predisposed toward an attitude of love. But this attitude is only possible when we believe that God loves us. Love is not our idea; it is God's. Because we are loved and secure, we can risk loving other people.

> **LOVE IS NOT OUR IDEA; IT'S GOD'S.**

*Love has been perfected among us in this: that we may have boldness in the day of judgment; because as He is, so are we in this world. There is no fear in love; but perfect love casts out fear, because fear involves torment. But he who fears has not been made perfect in love. We love Him because He first loved us.* (1 John 4:17–19)

Love is the answer to the foul stench of iniquity that gives entry to the enemy's warring ways and tactics. James said that lusts of mortal flesh literally *"war in [our] members"* (James 4:1). When we are born again and receive the Holy Spirit, God helps us overcome our anti-love nature, but it is a daily battle that we must choose to fight. The battle lines are drawn around our families, the church, the workplace, the grocery store, the bank—wherever there is the possibility and opportunity to express the love of God.

## WALK IN HUMILITY

There has been much misunderstanding about humility. To be humble does not mean that we become doormats.

To walk in humility means that we have a proper concept of God and of our relationship to Him. Also remember that those sitting and working around you weekly in your New Testament church are vessels of God's Holy Spirit, just as you are. When we walk by the Spirit, in love and humility, we are able to *"overcome evil with good"* (Romans 12:21) and *"cover a multitude of sins"* (James 5:20; 1 Peter 4:8). We are able to walk in grace, both receiving and extending it to others.

> *But He gives more grace. Therefore He says: "God resists the proud, but gives grace to the humble." Therefore submit to God. Resist the devil and he will flee from you. Draw near to God and He will draw near to you. Cleanse your hands, you sinners; and purify your hearts, you double-minded. Lament and mourn and weep! Let your laughter be turned to mourning and your joy to gloom. Humble yourselves in the sight of the Lord, and He will lift you up.* (James 4:6–10)

God gives us *"more grace"*—as much as we need. God gives us more of Himself as we resist the devil and draw near to God. God lifts us up as we humble ourselves toward His throne. As we walk by the Spirit, in love and humility, we walk in the same grace that saved us, giving glory and honor to God.

# Chapter Six

## Taking Our Stand against the Enemy

# Chapter Six

# Taking Our Stand against the Enemy

*Finally, my brethren, be strong in the Lord and in the power of His might. Put on the whole armor of God, that you may be able to stand against the wiles of the devil.*
—Ephesians 6:10–11

There is no better example for how to live our lives as Christ's followers than Christ Himself. This makes perfect sense, yet we so frequently forget it and try to be Christlike without even looking first at the life of our Lord!

This holds true in all realms, including the realm of standing against the enemy. Jesus knows firsthand what it is like to undergo temptation and we should consider how He handled temptation when we face temptation ourselves. As Hebrews 4:15 reminds us, *"We do not have a High Priest who cannot sympathize with our weaknesses, but was in all points tempted as we are, yet without sin."*

Do you remember the Lord's wilderness experience? The call of ministry was heavy upon Him as John baptized Him, and then our Lord was led by the Spirit into the wilderness, where He was to be tempted by Satan. Just as Satan is eager to attack us today, he was all too ready to take on the challenge of tempting Christ on that day as well!

After Christ had been the in wilderness fasting for quite some time, the enemy made his move. Realizing that Christ was vulnerable and weakened with hunger, Satan tried enticing the Savior to succumb to lusts of the eye, lusts of the flesh, and pridefulness.

He first sought to play upon Jesus' hunger, insisting that Jesus prove his position in the kingdom by turning stones into bread. Christ, having spent time in his Father's presence, drew the sword of the Spirit to contend with His enemy, saying, *"It is written, 'Man shall not live by bread alone, but by every word that proceeds from the mouth of God'"* (Matthew 4:4).

Satan, seeing Jesus to be a worthy opponent, hurled another temptation at Him. He took Jesus to a high pinnacle and encouraged Him to throw Himself down, using distorted Scripture to convince Christ that it was a good idea, saying,

> *If You are the Son of God, throw Yourself down. For it is written: "He shall give His angels charge over you," and, "In their hands they shall bear you up, Lest you dash your foot against a stone."* (Matthew 4:6)

Again, Jesus was ready to strike back with the Word. *"It is written again,"* He said, *"'You shall not tempt the LORD your God'"* (verse 7).

The enemy, unhappy yet still too stubborn and prideful to accept defeat, took Jesus up a high mountain and showed Him all the kingdoms of the world. In his arrogance, the enemy said to Jesus, *"All these things I will give You if You will fall down and worship me"* (verse 9).

> SATAN OFTEN ATTACKS WHEN WE ARE MOST VULNERABLE.

Christ, tired of the enemy's games, let the devil have it once more by fighting back with Scripture. *"Away with you, Satan! For it is written, 'You shall worship the LORD your God, and Him only you shall serve'"* (verse 10). Finally, Satan left the Savior in efforts to recuperate from the battle and plan his next assault.

What do we learn from this passage? For one, we can see that Satan often chooses to attack when we are in our most vulnerable state. With Jesus, for instance, He waited until the Savior was weak with physical hunger before tempting Him to turn stone into bread. Satan still works the same way. He frequently waits until we are worn down, tired from other challenges, temptations, and trials, before he begins his assaults.

We also learn the key to standing strong against these assaults. Notice how Christ defeated Satan: He quoted Scripture. Even in His weakened state, Jesus was able to defeat Satan because He knew where to go for strength. He turned to His Father and His Father's Word, the Scriptures.

It would have been easy for Jesus to try to fight the battle on His own. How often do we try to "go it alone" when it comes to spiritual battles? Jesus could have easily done the same, but He turned to His Father and His Father's Word to help fight the battle. If Jesus, the very Son of God, turned to His Father and to Scriptures for help, shouldn't we do the same?

The apostle Paul told us that we are to *"stand against the wiles of the devil."* If we are to stand against the enemy, it will not be in our own strength. We can only be *"strong in the Lord and in the power of His might."* Warring against the enemy in our own strength is like sending a bunch of toddlers against an armored division. But in God we have not only protection, but also a means by which to attack and dismantle the strongholds of the enemy.

# BE STRONG IN THE LORD

The key to dealing with the schemes of the enemy is to depend on the Lord rather than our own ability to defeat or outsmart him. It is by the grace of God alone that Satan is defeated. We will not overcome him with our own might and reason; the devil will not be reasonable, and, in reality, we possess nothing in ourselves with which to dispatch him. We must respect his power and call upon the wisdom of God to defeat him. Even the mighty archangel of God respected the power of Satan. As the book of Jude says, *"Michael the archangel, in contending with the devil, when he disputed about the body of Moses, dared not bring against him a reviling accusation, but said, 'The Lord rebuke you!'"* (Jude 9). If those who stand by the throne of God allow God to deal with Satan, then we probably should as well.

The word translated as *"wiles"* in Ephesians 6:11 is *methodeia,* from which we get our word *method.* A method is a predictable pattern that leads to a specific objective. Satan uses methods, which we have referred to as terrorism, psychological warfare, and overwhelming force, that, if allowed to continue, will divert glory from God.

Though we are involved in a violent battle, we have the assurance that the enemy ultimately will not prevail. We know from the Bible that the enemy is destined for destruction. For all his methods and tactics, he will ultimately fail.

*The devil, who deceived them, was cast into the lake of fire and brimstone where the beast and the false prophet are. And they will be tormented day and night forever and ever.* (Revelation 20:10)

In the meantime, Satan is determined to oppress and destroy as many lives as possible. So, to effectively deal with the tactics of Satan, we must first understand that our battle is not one of the flesh, but of the spirit. We cannot win a spiritual battle by carnal means (using our own strength and intelligence). We will wear ourselves out by warring with our natural minds, and we will always lose. This is why 2 Corinthians 10:4 says, *"For the weapons of our warfare are not carnal but mighty in God for pulling down strongholds."*

**OUR ABILITY IN SPIRITUAL WARFARE IS BY THE GRACE OF GOD.**

We have spent the previous chapters uncovering Satan's motives and methods. But unless we take Satan's deliberate and predictable strategy into account, he will take advantage of our ignorance and make us part of his plan. (See 2 Corinthians 2:11.) So now that we know what the enemy is up to, we can respond to his tactics by using what God has provided for this purpose.

The apostle Paul told us that we must *"stand against...the devil."* This seems like a contradiction. How do we defeat an enemy by standing? To say that we stand, however, is to say that we are warring in the enabling grace of God rather than by human means. Just as we can make no boast about our salvation by grace, neither can we boast of our own ability in our warfare. Both are accomplished by the grace of God through Jesus Christ.

# THE ARMOR OF GOD

In Paul's instructions in Ephesians 6, he told us that as we take our stand against the enemy, we must put on the *"whole armor of God."* He further explained which things we must *"put on"* and which things we must *"take up."* There are three things we *wear* and three things with which we *war.*

> *Finally, my brethren, be strong in the Lord and in the power of His might. Put on the whole armor of God, that you may be able to stand against the wiles of the devil. For we do not wrestle against flesh and blood, but against principalities, against powers, against the rulers of the darkness of this age, against spiritual hosts of wickedness in the heavenly places. Therefore take up the whole armor of God, that you may be able to withstand in the evil day, and having done all, to stand. Stand therefore, having girded your waist with truth, having put on the breastplate of righteousness, and having shod your feet with the preparation of the gospel of peace; above all, taking the shield of faith with which you will be able to quench all the fiery darts of the wicked one. And take the helmet of salvation, and the sword of the Spirit, which is the word of God; praying always with all prayer and supplication in the Spirit, being watchful to this end with all perseverance and supplication for all the saints; and for me.* (Ephesians 6:10–19)

The epistle to the Ephesians uses the words *"in Christ"* or their equivalent more than twenty times. Being "in

Christ" means that we belong to Him, that we have sub-mitted ourselves to Him as Lord. When Paul told us to put on the whole armor of God, he was referring to aspects of our being in Christ.

Ephesians 6:10–18 refers to six different items of armor that enable us to stand against the enemy's tactics. The first three items of our armor are related to our position in Christ. We have the *"truth"* of Christ, the *"righteousness"* of Christ, and the *"peace"* of Christ. These are all things that we must *"put on"* if we are to stand against the enemy. Galatians 3:27 tells us that if we have been baptized into Christ, then we have *"put on Christ."* These are the things we wear in Christ.

# THE BELT OF TRUTH

All of the enemy's tactics depend upon deception and lies. Satan sprinkles just enough truth over his poison to draw his victims. As a result, many of God's children have bought into his lies. When a small mistruth is accepted, Satan adds another and then another until only the lie remains.

Jesus said that Satan was a liar from the beginning:

*He was a murderer from the beginning, and does not stand in the truth, because there is no truth in him. When he speaks a lie, he speaks from his own resources, for he is a liar and the father of it.* (John 8:44)

The word for truth, *aletheia*, refers to what is true versus what is not true; to what is real versus what is false.

When we talk about having "girded our waists with truth," we are saying that if we are to stand against the enemy, we must prepare ourselves with the truth. To be prepared with truth means to be filled with the Scriptures. When we have filled ourselves with Scriptures, we are able to detect the deception of the enemy. The enemy's tactics of intimidation, manipulation, and domination cannot take us by surprise. When he tries to intimidate us, we remind him of the truth that God is in control. When he tries to manipulate our thoughts, we take those thoughts captive to the truth in Christ Jesus. When he tries to dominate us or dominate others through us, we remind ourselves of the truth that we live under the authority of Christ.

> TO STAND AGAINST THE ENEMY, WE MUST PREPARE OURSELVES WITH TRUTH.

When Satan confronted Jesus in the wilderness, Jesus defeated him with the Word of God from the Torah and the Psalms. Jesus could have brought twelve legions of angels onto the scene (Matthew 26:53), but He overcame the enemy with three words: *"It is written"* (Matthew 4:4, 7, 10). Each time Satan manipulated and misquoted the Scriptures (and Satan can quote the Scriptures), Jesus spoke the truth of God's Word and removed the ground upon which Satan tried to stand. Satan had to leave Him alone.

Jesus gave us the pattern to follow. Don't fight hand to hand with the devil; instead, *"submit to God. Resist the devil and he will flee from you"* (James 4:7). Truth can and must be appropriated from the Scriptures if we are to defeat the lies of the devil. We must gird, or prepare ourselves, with the truth that we are in Christ.

# THE BREASTPLATE OF RIGHTEOUSNESS

A second item that we put on is the righteousness of Christ. We need to remember whose armor we are wearing—it belongs to Christ. So first we prepare ourselves for battle with the truth of God's Word, and then we put on the righteousness of Christ.

We cannot earn righteousness (right standing before God). One of the lies of the devil is that we must work *for* salvation. In reality, we only work *out* our salvation (Philippians 2:12). The enemy, though, tries to keep us distracted so that we don't *"occupy"* the world for the kingdom of God (Luke 19:13 KJV).

God gives us His own righteousness by the blood of Jesus Christ. We have been *"justified* [made right with God] *by faith, we have peace with God through our Lord Jesus Christ"* (Romans 5:1). When we wear the righteousness of Christ, we are not crippled and preoccupied by trying to work for what God has already freely given us. We are able to stand in the righteousness of Jesus Christ and pursue His purpose.

Putting on the breastplate of righteousness means that we go into battle with confidence in what Jesus Christ has done for us. Note that the breastplate covers our hearts. When we don the breastplate of Christ's righteousness, we are able to stand with confidence each time the enemy tries to keep us busy with thoughts about our own unworthiness. We stand wearing the worthiness of Jesus Christ. When the enemy tries to manipulate us by planting doubts as to our salvation and relationship with Christ, we can show him a blood-soaked cross and an empty tomb.

# THE GOSPEL OF PEACE

Now, having put on the *truth* of who we are in Christ and having been clothed with the *righteousness* of Christ, we put on the *peace* of Christ. Having our feet shod with the Good News of peace in Christ means that we are able to walk, or live, a life of peace in Christ. The Hebrew word for peace, *shalom*, means wholeness. It is in Christ that we are made whole. The enemy may taunt us with plaguing fears or bring up our past sin and failure, but all of these and more are settled in Christ Jesus.

Peace comes from the presence of the Holy Spirit and allows us to live effectively in the midst of turmoil. The peace of God surpasses human understanding, allowing us to know that God has everything in hand. Peace is the bequest of Jesus Christ to all those who trust Him.

*Peace I leave with you, My peace I give to you; not as the world gives do I give to you. Let not your heart be troubled, neither let it be afraid.* (John 14:27)

and,

*These things I have spoken to you, that in Me you may have peace. In the world you will have tribulation; but be of good cheer, I have overcome the world.*

(John 16:33)

In Christ we are neither in fear nor in trouble. He has removed all cause for fear. He has overcome every

**CHRIST HAS REMOVED ALL CAUSE FOR FEAR.**

weapon and strategy of the enemy by His own blood. It is inevitable that we will encounter the schemes of the enemy, but Christ has made it possible for us to walk and live in the peace of our position in Christ.

So there are three things that we put on in order to stand against the enemy: the *truth* of who we are in Christ, the *righteousness* of Christ, and the *peace* of Christ. There are now three things that we must *"take up"* to war against the enemy.

# THE SHIELD OF FAITH

A shield is something that we stand behind to protect us from the enemy's attack. It must be taken into the hand. Paul told us that we use this shield of faith to extinguish the fiery darts that the enemy throws at us. What are these darts? They are the very tactics and strategies of the enemy that we have discussed in this book. They are his strategies of terror, psychological warfare, and overwhelming force.

Taking up the shield of faith is trusting in all the things we just spoke of: putting on truth, righteousness, and peace in Christ.

Faith is the gateway to the enabling grace of God. We are saved by grace through faith (Ephesians 2:8). We also war by grace through faith. The one who trusts or depends on the Lord trusts in what He has said in His Word.

> *As for God, His way is perfect; the word of the LORD is proven; He is a shield to all who trust in Him.*
> (Psalm 18:30)

and,

> *Those who trust in the LORD are like Mount Zion, which cannot be moved, but abides forever.* (Psalm 125:1)

and,

> *Every word of God is pure; He is a shield to those who put their trust in Him.* (Proverbs 30:5)

and,

> *You will keep him in perfect peace, whose mind is stayed on You, because he trusts in You. Trust in the LORD forever, for in YAH, the LORD, is everlasting strength.* (Isaiah 26:3–4)

and,

> *Blessed is the man who trusts in the LORD, and whose hope is the LORD. For he shall be like a tree planted by*

*the waters, which spreads out its roots by the river, and will not fear when heat comes; but its leaf will be green, and will not be anxious in the year of drought, nor will cease from yielding fruit.* (Jeremiah 17:7–8)

If we are to stand against the enemy, we must believe in all that we have put on in Jesus Christ.

# THE HELMET OF SALVATION

When Paul spoke about putting on the helmet of salvation, he was referring to protecting our minds. Hope is the anticipation of God's goodness. When we take up the helmet of salvation, we are filling our minds with the hope that it is God's intention to redeem and save all people everywhere.

The helmet of salvation is linked in Scripture with hope and deliverance.

*He saw that there was no man, and wondered that there was no intercessor; therefore His own arm brought salvation for Him; and His own righteousness, it sustained Him. For He put on righteousness as a breastplate, and a helmet of salvation on His head; He put on the garments of vengeance for clothing, and was clad with zeal as a cloak.* (Isaiah 59:16–17)

and,

*But let us who are of the day be sober, putting on the breastplate of faith and love, and as a helmet the hope of salvation.* (1 Thessalonians 5:8)

As we war against the enemy, we do so knowing that it is God's intention to redeem all of creation. Isaiah 59 refers to God's deliverance of Israel, but it also speaks prophetically of Jesus Christ in His vengeance against the enemies of God. Jesus was born to destroy the works and tactics of the enemy (1 John 3:8). We read that all of creation groans with this reality (Romans 8:22). It is

> HOPE IS THE ANTICIPATION OF GOD'S GOODNESS.

with this hope that we wage war against the enemy. It is through knowing this reality that we can wage a confident war against Satan. Setbacks may come, but the war is already won, and those in Christ are on the winning side.

On D-Day, June 6, 1944, the Allied armies landed at Normandy. It took them a long time to establish a beachhead and then move into the land to rout the forces of Nazi Germany. Though the war would go on for another year, Hitler's fate was sealed on D-Day. So it is with Satan. There are battles yet to be fought; there will still be causalities; but the outcome has never been in doubt. The cross of Christ was Satan's D-Day, and the "D" in this case stands for his defeat.

If we are to stand against the enemy, we must be sure of God's heart and intention. His heart is focused on salvation and His intention is to fill the earth with His glory. When we are confident of this, we can stand unaffected by the distractions of the enemy.

> *But truly, as I live, all the earth shall be filled with the*
> *glory of the LORD.* (Numbers 14:21)

# THE SWORD OF THE WORD

The last article with which we war is the Word of God. The Greek word translated as *"word"* is *rhema*. The *rhema* of God is the Spirit-activated and inspired Word. It is the declaration of Scripture to address specific situations and obstacles. Here, we are referring to the Word of God being spoken against the power and strongholds of the enemy. It is the Word, the *rhema*, that destroys those prideful things lifted up against God referred to in 2 Corinthians 10. So how do we handle this sword? Through our mouths.

*And He has made My mouth like a sharp sword.*
(Isaiah 49:2)

and,

*For the word of God is living and powerful, and sharper than any two-edged sword, piercing even to the division of soul and spirit, and of joints and marrow, and is a discerner of the thoughts and intents of the heart.*
(Hebrews 4:12)

The Word of God is called the sword of the Spirit because it can be spoken under the inspiration of the Holy Spirit to address a specific issue. When the enemy speaks fear, the Word speaks faith. When the enemy speaks failure, the Word speaks purpose. When the enemy speaks diversion, the Word speaks devotion. In all, the *rhema* of God is wielded as an offensive weapon to cut down the enemy tactics that distract and divert us from fellowship with God.

With all the articles of God's armor in place, we are able to stand against Satan. As we wear and war with all God has provided, we destroy the power of the enemy to the glory and honor of God.

# DISCERNMENT

*Praying always with all prayer and supplication in the Spirit, being watchful to this end with all perseverance and supplication for all the saints.*

(Ephesians 6:18)

Now that we know what the enemy is doing and the countermeasures we have in Christ, we need to be able to recognize when Satan is prowling about. To this end, God gives us discernment, so that we might live godly lives in an antichrist world system. Worldly lust, carnality, and false teaching bombard us every day. We are virtually surrounded by enemy activity everywhere we go—and we need discernment to overcome it.

All of us exercise discernment to one degree or another. Sometimes we have a "feeling" that something is "just not right." We can't put a finger on why, but somehow an inner voice, an inner knowing, lets us know. We may reason that this feeling is only a coincidence or something from our rational minds when, in fact, what is at work is discernment.

# THE BATTLE FOR THE MIND

There is a conflict going on in the battleground of our minds. It is a war between flesh and spirit, between obedience and disobedience. One leads toward death and the other toward life and peace in God. If we are in a situation and have to question our motivation, then the fact that we even had to ask ourselves the source of our thoughts or feelings may be an indication that all is not as it should be. If I have to ask myself whether or not something is true, then it may be untrue in some aspect.

Paul told us that there are two directions in which we can set our minds.

> *For those who live according to the flesh set their minds on the things of the flesh, but those who live according to the Spirit, the things of the Spirit. For to be carnally minded is death, but to be spiritually minded is life and peace. Because the carnal mind is enmity against God.*
> (Romans 8:5–7)

Satan, operating through the flesh, always leads us toward pleasing ourselves, while God always leads us toward pleasing Him. These two are as opposite as they can be. What is of God leads us to life and peace. What is of the flesh, motivated by iniquity, leads to separation from God, which leads to death. In John 8:44, Jesus described the devil as a *"murderer"* (one who robs us of life) and as a *"liar"* (in other words, he speaks for his own purposes of distraction and diversion from God).

Discernment is that "God part" of us that warns us when we come into a demonic setting. The children of God are able to sense the clashing of God's truth versus Satan's counterfeit. God's purpose in discernment is to allow us to participate in those things that are of God and to avoid the snares of the devil. Paul desired that we would walk in discernment and thus give no offense to God.

> *And this I pray, that your love may abound still more and more in knowledge and all discernment, that you may approve the things that are excellent, that you may be sincere and without offense till the day of Christ.*
> (Philippians 1:9–10)

We can clearly differentiate between what is from God and what is from the enemy by observing the attitude or direction of the words or thoughts involved. I would suggest a few "attitude indicators" here. The following is not a complete listing, but it includes some of the most obvious ones. Note the contrasting feelings that occur depending on whether God or the enemy is at work.

| The Enemy at Work | God at Work |
| --- | --- |
| I feel pushed. | I feel invited. |
| I feel panic. | I feel peace. |
| I feel confused. | I feel clarity. |
| I feel condemned. | I feel confronted. |
| I feel insecure. | I feel loved. |
| I feel powerless. | I feel confident. |

In addition to feelings or emotions, we also must examine the *character* of what we think and how we act. James gave us a way to determine the origin of our thoughts. Are they from God, or do they feed carnal lust?

*Who is wise and understanding among you? Let him show by good conduct that his works are done in the meekness of wisdom. But if you have bitter envy and self-seeking in your hearts, do not boast and lie against the truth. This wisdom does not descend from above, but is earthly, sensual, demonic. For where envy and self-seeking exist, confusion and every evil thing are there. But the wisdom that is from above is first pure, then peaceable, gentle, willing to yield, full of mercy and good fruits, without partiality and without hypocrisy. Now the fruit of righteousness is sown in peace by those who make peace.* (James 3:13–18)

James described the wisdom or thoughts that stem from our old carnal nature (inspired by the enemy) as bitter, envious, self-seeking, lying, earthly, sensual, demonic, confusing, and evil. On the other hand, he said the wisdom from God is pure, peaceable, gentle, yielding, merciful, fruitful, impartial, and honest. The contrast and the sources are clear. We are not responsible to hold on to the thoughts and attitudes that stem from the enemy's tactics. When we encounter thoughts that are not from God, we must respond by taking those thoughts

> WE MUST EXAMINE THE CHARACTER OF WHAT WE THINK AND HOW WE ACT.

captive, referring them back to God, and giving them no further consideration. We must refuse the enemy at the door and not let him into our houses.

*Now we have received, not the spirit of the world, but the Spirit who is from God, that we might know the things that have been freely given to us by God. These things we also speak, not in words which man's wisdom teaches but which the Holy Spirit teaches, comparing spiritual things with spiritual.*

(1 Corinthians 2:12–13)

# STAND FIRM

Take your stand against the enemy. Wrap yourself in the truth, righteousness, and peace of Jesus Christ. Speak the Word of God incisively in the face of the enemy. Remind him whose armor you are wearing while you stand firm against him.

*Now to Him who is able to keep you from stumbling, and to present you faultless before the presence of His glory with exceeding joy, to God our Savior, who alone is wise, be glory and majesty, dominion and power, both now and forever. Amen.* (Jude 24–25)

# Chapter Seven

## The Last Word on War

# Chapter Seven

## The Last Word on War

Spiritual warrior, understand this. When we are in the heat of battle, God isn't scratching His head trying to figure how He will bring us victory. He knows the war we are in; He brought us into the fray, and we are standing in His power and anointing. Even though we will encounter the devil everywhere we go, he is no match for the truth of God's Word. Remember, too, that as we grow and learn new levels in God, we also will encounter new resistance. It goes, according to a saying I've heard, "New level, new devil."

Despite this resistance, you can oppose evil with confidence because God's faithfulness and ability in battle have been proven throughout the millennia. Scripture is full of God's victories over Satan, as well as the victories of His followers.

These stories of victory can encourage us as we battle against unseen forces. They can build us up when we feel that defeat is imminent. Most importantly, they can show us where our power comes from and how unlimited that source, God, is.

Battle by battle, throughout Scripture and throughout the history of His church, God has shown and continues to show His true might. Even with all His victories, these battles are but a foretaste of the final victory at the end of the age, when Satan will be defeated one final time.

# MOSES VERSUS PHARAOH

When the Israelites were enslaved in Egypt, God sent Moses to deliver them. He had Moses perform various signs to convince Pharaoh of God's power and authenticity. At first, Pharaoh's magicians and astrologers performed similar signs, but God always showed Himself more powerful.

*So Moses and Aaron went in to Pharaoh, and they did so, just as the LORD commanded. And Aaron cast down his rod before Pharaoh and before his servants, and it became a serpent. But Pharaoh also called the wise men and the sorcerers; so the magicians of Egypt, they also did in like manner with their enchantments.*

*For every man threw down his rod, and they became*
*serpents. But Aaron's rod swallowed up their rods.*
(Exodus 7:10–12)

When this did not convince Pharaoh, God took things
up a notch and sent ten plagues. The
magicians felt they were equal to the
plagues of blood and of frogs, but
when God sent lice, even the magicians
had to admit that the power working
through Moses was greater than any
trick of theirs.

> **BATTLE BY
> BATTLE,
> GOD HAS
> SHOWN HIS
> TRUE MIGHT.**

*Now the magicians so worked with their enchantments*
*to bring forth lice, but they could not. So there were*
*lice on man and beast. Then the magicians said to Pha-*
*raoh, "This is the finger of God."*   (Exodus 8:18–19)

From this point on, the magicians are not mentioned
again. They were no longer able to duplicate the plagues
God sent, and perhaps they even stopped trying.

When Moses took on Pharaoh's astrologers and
magicians, the power of God humiliated them with an
utter defeat.

# ELIJAH VERSUS BAAL

In the great showdown between Elijah and the prophets of Baal on Mount Carmel, God sent fire from heaven to
show His power in Israel. The prophets of Baal called on
their god for hours, shouting and cutting themselves with

swords, with no results. But when Elijah called on the true God, things went differently.

First Elijah repaired the ruined altar of the Lord, rebuilding it with twelve stones—one for each of the Israelite tribes. Then he placed the wood and his sacrifice on the altar. At this point, he was expected to call on God to burn the sacrifice, but he wasn't done yet. He ordered four large jars of water to be poured on the sacrifice and on the wood. When this was done, he asked for four more jars, and then again for four more. Scripture says that the water ran down around the altar, even filling the trench around it. Then Elijah prayed a simple prayer.

> *Elijah the prophet came near and said, "LORD God of Abraham, Isaac, and Israel, let it be known this day that You are God in Israel and I am Your servant, and that I have done all these things at Your word. Hear me, O LORD, hear me, that this people may know that You are the LORD God, and that You have turned their hearts back to You again." Then the fire of the LORD fell and consumed the burnt sacrifice, and the wood and the stones and the dust, and it licked up the water that was in the trench.*
>
> (1 Kings 18:36–38)

God answered Elijah's prayer. He made it known that He was God, and that day the people fell on their faces, saying, *"The LORD, He is God! The LORD, He is God"* (verse 39).

# THE HEBREW CHILDREN VERSUS NEBUCHADNEZZAR'S COURT

After Nebuchadnezzar, the king of Babylon, overthrew Jerusalem, he asked for any promising young men who were strong and intelligent to be brought to the king's palace to serve at his court and be assimilated into Babylonian culture. Daniel and his friends Hananiah, Mishael, and Azariah were some of these promising men. However, not only were they strong and intelligent, as Nebuchadnezzar had required, they were also determined to continue living by God's laws rather than the laws of their new home. When they were brought food from the king's table, they refused to be defiled (the first portion of the king's food was offered to idols and therefore contaminated) and instead chose to eat vegetables. Because of their continual obedience, God blessed them with wisdom and knowledge.

When they were brought to Nebuchadnezzar's court so that Nebuchadnezzar could interview them, God demonstrated to the king that His power was ten times greater than the power of his magicians and astrologers, who used power from Satan.

> *Then the king interviewed them, and among them all none was found like Daniel, Hananiah, Mishael, and Azariah; therefore they served before the king. And in all matters of wisdom and understanding about which the king examined them, he found them ten times better than all the magicians and astrologers who were in all his realm.* (Daniel 1:19–20)

131

# PHILIP, PETER, AND JOHN VERSUS SIMON

In the earliest days of the church, Christians were persecuted harshly. As a result, the apostles and followers of Christ were often scattered throughout Roman territory and beyond. During such a time of scattering, Philip started a crusade in the city of Samaria.

Samaria was the city where the wicked queen Jezebel instituted Baal worship in Israel. (See 1 Kings 16:29–32.) Elijah destroyed her prophets and mocked Satan's worship nine hundred years before Philip brought the Gospel into the city. But by the time Philip arrived, Satan's witchcraft had re-rooted and many of its inhabitants were under curses or spells. That is, until Philip entered, and later John and Peter.

> *Then Philip went down to the city of Samaria and preached Christ to them. And the multitudes with one accord heeded the things spoken by Philip, hearing and seeing the miracles which he did. For unclean spirits, crying with a loud voice, came out of many who were possessed; and many who were paralyzed and lame were healed. And there was great joy in that city.*
> (Acts 8:5–8)

Now, there was a great sorcerer named Simon living in Samaria at the time (the same one we discussed earlier). After he heard that the Spirit of God had delivered many from demon possession and physical sickness, he wanted to find out about and obtain this power that was greater than his.

Simon had seen the demonstration of God's power and received the Gospel; he had believed and was baptized. However, when Peter and John came down from Jerusalem to minister to Samaria's converts, Simon sought to buy God's power.

Peter rebuked Simon's gall and iniquity, driving the new convert in prayer to his knees, saying, *"Pray to the Lord for me, that none of the things which you have spoken may come upon me"* (Acts 8:24).

Judging from Simon's fear and from his strong desire to buy the power of the Holy Spirit, we can only assume that God's power was greater than any he had seen before.

## PAUL VERSUS ELYMAS

God will let His Word be heard by those who desire to hear it, no matter what evil forces stand in the way. When Elymas the sorcerer opposed Paul on the island of Paphos, trying to prevent Paul from sharing the Gospel with his fellow sorcerer, the Spirit of God struck Elymas blind.

*Now when they had gone through the island to Paphos, they found a certain sorcerer, a false prophet, a Jew whose name was Bar-Jesus, who was with the proconsul, Sergius Paulus, an intelligent man. This man called for Barnabas and Saul and sought to hear the word of God. But Elymas the sorcerer (for so his name is translated) withstood them, seeking to turn the proconsul away from the faith. Then Saul, who also is called Paul, filled with the Holy Spirit, looked intently at him and said, "O full of all deceit and all fraud, you son of the devil, you enemy of all righteousness, will you not cease perverting the straight ways of the Lord? And now, indeed, the hand of the Lord is upon you, and you shall be blind, not seeing the sun for a time." And immediately a dark mist fell on him, and he went around seeking someone to lead him by the hand. Then the proconsul believed, when he saw what had been done, being astonished at the teaching of the Lord. (Acts 13:6–12)*

GOD WILL LET HIS WORD BE HEARD BY THOSE WHO DESIRE TO HEAR IT.

Paul was doing God's will when he encountered this practitioner of witchcraft. When the sorcerer came against him, the Holy Spirit empowered Paul's words and he was the victor.

# PAUL AND SILAS VERSUS THE CRAFT

When Paul and Silas ministered in Philipi, they met a slave girl possessed with a spirit of divination. Remember, divination is the practice of using the stars and evil spirits to foretell the future.

*Now it happened, as we went to prayer, that a certain slave girl possessed with a spirit of divination met us, who brought her masters much profit by fortune-telling.*

*This girl followed Paul and us, and cried out, saying,
"These men are the servants of the Most High God,
who proclaim to us the way of salvation." And this she
did for many days. But Paul, greatly annoyed, turned
and said to the spirit, "I command you in the name
of Jesus Christ to come out of her." And he came out
that very hour. But when her masters saw that their
hope of profit was gone, they seized Paul and Silas and
dragged them into the marketplace to the authorities.*
(Acts 16:16–19)

This fortune-teller, as we would call her today, worked
for a group of men who marketed her services. But when
Paul cast out the evil spirits from this girl, she could no
longer see the future. Once he detected the girl's demonic
disturbance, he declared, *"I command you in the name of
Jesus Christ to come out of her!"* And the girl was free. That's
power.

# THE BATTLE IS WON

These accounts serve to show us the power God has
invested in His church to destroy Satan's works. They also
show us what happens when the demonic hosts of witchcraft are confronted by the power of God. As you continue
to study the Scriptures closely, you can see how God's
power has been resident throughout history to destroy
Satan's power.

As saints of the Most High God, we should know that
the hand of God is always with us. We must allow our

prayers to ascend into heaven as incense every day. And we should pray for, support, and exhort others who stand up against Satan and his demonic kingdom.

As Christians, we have the gift and ability—through Christ—to cast out devils and destroy Satan's works. It's time to use it.

# Chapter Eight

# Before the Throne of God

# Chapter Eight

# Before the Throne of God

We began Chapter One by describing a scene at the throne of God. Lucifer, the anointed cherub, was distracted by his own beauty and turned away from God. In that moment, the crookedness of iniquity was born. The serpent then infected man with this same diversionary crookedness at the Fall. Man believed Satan's lie that he could *"be like God"* (Genesis 5:3).

Lucifer, now Satan the accuser, uses strategies of *intimidation, manipulation,* and *domination* to draw us away from

God. He works these strategies in us and sometimes through us to rob God of our fellowship and worship. Regardless of the particular strategy he uses, the enemy's objective is to shift our attention from God to ourselves. It is important to note, once again, that all sin is not the result of direct satanic involvement. Some of it is the influence of our iniquitous old nature, which is innately prone to sin. To ascribe all sin to Satan is to give him too much glory.

We have seen how the enemy's strategies work. We have learned how to stand against him by putting on the armor of God in Christ Jesus. As we conclude this study, we bring the issues of iniquity and warfare full circle, back to the throne where it all began. Why? We must understand that the war we fight is ultimately won at the throne of God. Our victory is by God's sovereign grace. Regardless of our efforts or obedience, our restoration is the product of God's love and compassion.

> OUR RESTORATION IS THE PRODUCT OF GOD'S LOVE AND COMPASSION.

# CHANGING CLOTHES IN HEAVEN'S COURT

The prophet Zechariah described a scene that demonstrates a change in our nature from one of uncleanness to one of holiness by God's own design. The throne room where iniquity was born now becomes a courtroom where it is removed.

*Then he showed me Joshua the high priest standing before the Angel of the LORD, and Satan standing at his right hand to oppose him. And the LORD said to Satan, "The LORD rebuke you, Satan! The LORD who has chosen Jerusalem rebuke you! Is this not a brand plucked from the fire?" Now Joshua was clothed with filthy garments, and was standing before the Angel. Then He answered and spoke to those who stood before Him, saying, "Take away the filthy garments from him." And to him He said, "See, I have removed your iniquity from you, and I will clothe you with rich robes." And I said, "Let them put a clean turban on his head." So they put a clean turban on his head, and they put the clothes on him. And the Angel of the LORD stood by.* (Zechariah 3:1–5)

As we enter the scene, we see Joshua standing before the throne of God. He stands as a priest in proxy for the nation of Israel, which had departed from God. In another sense, Joshua represents all of us who draw near to God by the blood of Jesus Christ. He stands before the throne in clothes stained as with dung. These stains represent the iniquity that separates man from God. Each stain represents a step off the path of God's ways.

# WE ARE CHARGED

The accuser stands by us to bring charges against us. Satan is a legalist; he's the prosecuting attorney in heaven's courtroom. He knows the law well. It is he who roams the earth looking for those he might accuse before God, as he did with Job. (See Job 1:6–11; 2:1–5.) He loves to whisper the record of our sin in our ears to bring shame and cause us to hide from God. Ironically, he inspires the very deeds that he now presents as evidence against us. He points to each stain on our robes, reminding us that we listened to him. *"Adultery, fornication, uncleanness, lewdness, idolatry, sorcery, hatred, contentions, jealousies, outbursts of wrath, selfish ambitions, dissensions, heresies, envy, murders, drunkenness, revelries"* (Galatians 5:19–21)—these are the charges that the accuser brings against us. And what is worse, he is telling the truth! We are all guilty before the bench of heaven's court.

We stand before God as *"unclean...and all our righteousnesses are like filthy rags"* (Isaiah 64:6). Just as his praise filled the halls of heaven in eternity past, now the accuser spews forth the fruit of his own treason before God. As Satan drones his list of infractions, the Lord stops him with a sudden rebuke. The Lord declares to the accuser, "Enough! Enough! God has chosen man to abide with Him." God has seen our deeds of the flesh and has chosen to be gracious to us. He has seen our dung-spattered rags, yet, in His mercy, He smothers Satan's railing account. "Enough!"

# WE ARE CHANGED

As we stand before the throne, the Lord issues His decree: "Take off those filthy rags and put royal robes on him." In an instant, our contemptible clothing is removed from us at God's command. This is more than a temporary change of wardrobe; it is the permanent removal of the iniquity that has controlled us since that moment in the Garden, thousands of years ago. Our filth is removed to the trash heap, and we stand before God restored.

We do not stand naked in heaven, however. God orders the attendants of heaven's court to place a priestly crown on our heads. God begins the process of renewing our minds so that we might live holy in this new state of glory. Instead of our thoughts being filled with self, they are now focused on God and His glory. Then God orders that royal, festive robes be put on us—robes of celebration and praise. Note that it is not we who clothe ourselves, but it is the Lord who covers us. It is not by our effort or perfection that we stand in God's presence; it is by His decision alone. We are clothed with His righteousness simply because He loves us and wants us there.

> GOD TAKES OFF OUR FILTHY RAGS AND DRESSES US IN ROYAL ROBES.

We no longer live according to the spattered rags that we wore. We are no longer bound to walk that crooked trail blazed by our fathers. We *"have no obligation whatever to [our] old sinful nature to do what it begs [us] to do"* (Romans 8:12 TLB). Instead, we have access to the throne of God in the Spirit. We are free to be devoted to God, to worship without distraction at His throne. We are restored to that place of fellowship that Adam enjoyed with God at first. Satan's rebellion has been crushed!

Now restored to God, we can turn aside the tactics of Satan and refuse to be employed in his designs. When that desire of our old nature wells up to attack another, we can say "No!" Now, when we are given a door to watch (like the lady usher I spoke of), we no longer guard it as our own possession, but keep it as an act of worship to the Lord.

# PEACE DECLARED

How can this be? Zechariah told us that it is by the *"BRANCH."* *"For behold, I am bringing forth My Servant the BRANCH"* (Zechariah 3:8). The "BRANCH" is the Lord Jesus Himself, who was cast into the bitter waters of our iniquity to sweeten them.

God is a holy God, and He cannot abide defilement of any sort. His holiness demands perfection—a perfection that we are unable to supply. God says, *"By those who come near Me I must be regarded as holy; and before all the people I must be glorified"* (Leviticus 10:3). Since we are incapable of being holy or providing holiness, God has provided His own righteousness and holiness for us. The prophet Isaiah said, *"His own arm brought salvation for Him; and His own righteousness, it sustained Him"* (Isaiah 59:16).

Jesus hung on the tree, suspended between earth and glory. By the Cross He removed the curse of our iniquity and paid for each stain of our sin. We enter into His finished work through repentance and faith toward God.

The curse of iniquity is removed by confessing and believing in God's provision in Christ Jesus.

> *That if you confess with your mouth the Lord Jesus and believe in your heart that God has raised Him from the dead, you will be saved. For with the heart one believes unto righteousness, and with the mouth confession is made unto salvation.*
> (Romans 10:9–10)

and,

> *Christ has redeemed us from the curse of the law, having become a curse for us (for it is written, "Cursed is everyone who hangs on a tree"), that the blessing of Abraham might come upon the Gentiles in Christ Jesus, that we might receive the promise of the Spirit through faith.* (Galatians 3:13–14)

Jesus became a curse on the cross so we could evict the devil from our lives and destroy iniquity. He was wounded so we could be healed. He took upon Himself all the sins of the world with us in mind. He has brought healing to our hearts and enabled us to live a God-pleasing life before the throne of God.

> *Beloved, if our heart does not condemn us, we have confidence toward God. And whatever we ask we receive from Him, because we keep His commandments and do those things that are pleasing in His sight.*
> (1 John 3:21–22)

Whatever we were, Jesus became our exchange. When we accept the fact that Jesus is Lord to the glory of God the Father, and when we take captive the devil's lies to the truth of God, Satan must scamper out of the courtroom in Jesus' name!

# LIVING BEFORE THE THRONE

The Lord tells us that there are two facets to our living before the throne of God in this restored state. He said, *"If you will walk in My ways,"* and *"If you will keep My command"* (Zechariah 3:7).

# WALKING IN HIS WAYS

Even we believers have walked in our own ways. In other words, we have lived to please ourselves. You may say, "Wait a minute. I've done good things for God. I've gone to church and given of my money. I've served the Lord on this or that committee, and I handed out food to the needy." These and all the other things we do are good things. But *for whom* did we do them? Did we do them to appear righteous? Who has gotten the glory for all that we have done? Do we call attention to ourselves, even in a small way, as we do these good things? Do we ever look in the mirror to approve some new level of righteousness we

> GOD SHOULD NOT BE A SENTIMENTAL AFTERTHOUGHT, BUT RATHER THE FOCUS OF ALL WE DO.

have attained? Do we ever criticize anyone else for not doing the good things we have done? Do we delight in the recognition and status of titles we have attained in the church? Do we ever do these good things anonymously? These are some hard questions, but the answers will determine the actual motivation behind our lives and ministries.

When God tells us to walk in His ways, He is telling us that we are to live a "throne-ward" life. We are to live to please and glorify God. He is not a sentimental afterthought; rather, He is the focus of all that we do.

When a farmer plows a field, he fixes his eyes on a point at the end of the row. Then, as he plows, he moves straight toward that point. If he were to take his eyes off that distant point, he would plow a crooked line and end up planting crooked rows. Similarly, when we walk in the ways of God, we say that He is the point at which we are aiming. We are focused on God and His glory. We do not turn aside to grab a little recognition for ourselves. Each time we do walk in our own way, or live for ourselves, we plow in the crookedness of iniquity. When we are secure in Christ, however, we no longer have to grab anything for ourselves. We can walk straight toward Him in everything we do.

Jesus told us,

*When you do a charitable deed, do not let your left hand know what your right hand is doing, that your charitable deed may be in secret; and your Father*

*who sees in secret will Himself reward you openly.*
(Matthew 6:3–4)

To walk in the way of God is to fix our eyes upon Jesus and the throne of God. Remember that the basis for Satan's strategies is pleasing ourselves, admiring ourselves, and focusing on ourselves. But now, through Christ Jesus, we are free to center our lives on God, as before the Fall.

# KEEPING HIS COMMAND

To *"keep the command of the Lord"* (2 Chronicles 13:11) refers to living a life of listening to God. A command is something God has spoken to us. The lives of all who followed God in the Bible and in history were characterized by their listening to or hearing God and then responding in obedience. Abraham heard the voice of God and founded a family. Moses heard the voice of God and delivered a nation. Jesus heard the voice of the Father and redeemed the world. Keeping the command of God also requires that we realize we live in a dynamic relationship with God. God is always speaking and always moving, so we must always be listening and responding to what we hear.

When the Lord spoke to Joshua, the high priest, about keeping His command, He also was referring to the conduct of His house. God has established each of us in a ministry of His house. To follow the command of God, we must be faithful to and minister in the place where the Lord has established us. Many try to assume a place that God has not given them. The motivation for such ministry is not grounded in devotion to God and is not the result of hearing God but, rather, of following their own whims. This is perhaps one of the greatest areas of opportunity for Satan to influence the church. Even the great apostle Paul ministered in a particular *"sphere"* that God granted to him.

> *For we are not overextending ourselves (as though our authority did not extend to you), for it was to you that we came with the gospel of Christ; not boasting of things beyond measure, that is, in other men's labors, but having hope, that as your faith is increased, we shall be greatly enlarged by you in our sphere, to preach the gospel in the regions beyond you, and not to boast in another man's sphere of accomplishment. But "he who glories, let him glory in the LORD." For not he who commends himself is approved, but whom the Lord commends.* (2 Corinthians 10:14–18)

We must ask ourselves, "Where would God have us minister in the body of Christ?" God is calling and equipping us to minister in whatever true burdens He has put before us. Jesus did not go around ministering wherever and whatever He wanted. No, He spoke only the words of His Father and did only what He saw the Father doing. If we are living a "throne-ward" life, then the burdens of God will become ours as well, and we will minister in His enabling grace rather than from our own ability. Jesus

> GOD IS CALLING AND EQUIPPING US TO MINISTER IN WHATEVER BURDENS HE HAS PUT BEFORE US.

spoke of the correlation between relationship with God and ministry:

> *Then Jesus answered and said to them, "Most assuredly, I say to you, the Son can do nothing of Himself, but what He sees the Father do; for whatever He does, the Son also does in like manner. For the Father loves the Son, and shows Him all things that He Himself does; and He will show Him greater works than these, that you may marvel."* (John 5:19–20)

and,

> *Do you not believe that I am in the Father, and the Father in Me? The words that I speak to you I do not speak on My own authority; but the Father who dwells in Me does the works.* (John 14:10)

How will we know when we minister beyond our sphere—when we have not kept the command of the Lord? We will know it if we find ourselves pushing someone else aside to gain a position. We will know it when we begin to yearn for the titles men give to us rather than to please God. We will know it when we have no peace and no fruit born of our ministry. We will know it when we catch ourselves telling others in the body how important we are and calling ourselves by official titles. It is enough to serve the Lord. Jesus taught His disciples that we should wait to be asked to move up to another position at the table. He said, *"When you are invited, go and sit down in the lowest place, so that when he who invited you comes he may say to you, 'Friend, go up higher.' Then you will have glory*

*in the presence of those who sit at the table with you. For who-
ever exalts himself will be humbled, and he who humbles himself will be exalted"* (Luke 14:10–11). The same applies to
positions in the body of Christ. Bear in mind that, regardless of position, we are all still at the same table with the
Lord—and who is above Him?

When we have begun to live a "throne-ward," listening life before God, the Lord promises that there will be a
positive result.

# THE RESULTS OF LIVING BEFORE THE THRONE OF GOD

When we live a "throne-ward" and listening life, the
Lord says, *"Then you shall also judge My house, and likewise
have charge of My courts; I will give you places to walk among
these who stand here"* (Zechariah 3:7).

All three things mentioned in this verse can be
summed up in one word: *access.* The verse says that we
walk among those who stand before
the throne of heaven. This is another
way of saying that we live a life in
the Spirit. This is not a future event;
it is available to us now. We also
have access to God, walking in His
very presence. We go from glory to
glory, our lives becoming a reflection
of whose we are. Just as Lucifer reflected the glory of God
before time, so we stand before the throne of God mirror-
ing His glory. Thus every act of our lives becomes an act

> THE TRUTH CHANGES THINGS ONLY WHEN IT IS APPLIED.

of worship to God. This is as it was before the beginning, and it is now again in Christ Jesus.

# LIVING BEFORE THE THRONE

It is not enough to know the truth, however. The truth changes things only when it is applied. We must make it our total purpose to equip God's church with the truth. Only the truth brings freedom, and it does so when we continue in it (John 8:32). We cannot send the church into battle unarmed and ill equipped; we must know and walk in the truth.

No, the war is not ended. There will yet be violent confrontations with a powerful enemy. Jesus said that *"the kingdom of heaven suffers violence, and the violent take it by force"* (Matthew 11:12). The enemy will still try to divert us from fellowship with God.

But, *you are destined to live before the throne of God.* The victory has been won and the enemy's strategies uncovered! In Christ you are back where you belong—at the throne of God with nothing to separate you from His love. I pray that the Lord will enliven His Word to you and that you will join in the overwhelming victory in Christ Jesus (John 16:33). In the words of the apostle Paul,

> *Yet in all these things we are more than conquerors through Him who loved us. For I am persuaded that neither death nor life, nor angels nor principalities nor powers, nor things present nor things*

*to come, nor height nor depth, nor any other cre-
ated thing, shall be able to separate us from the
love of God which is in Christ Jesus our Lord.*
(Romans 8:37–39)

# Appendices

# Appendix A

# Satan's Devices

The Bible teaches us the complete story of eternity, from creation and man's fall to the redemption of man by the blood of Jesus Christ and the final defeat of the enemy. We, as believers, are familiar with how the story ends. Unfortunately, however, many of us don't know where the pitfalls are. We don't know where to be wary of booby traps set by Satan to keep us from our purpose and destiny.

Because we often do not realize the degree of Satan's cunning ingenuity, we are frequently unprepared for the battle we are called to fight against him and his dark forces. Consequently, we end up living defeated lives, thereby not fulfilling the ministry to which God has called us.

This is why it is so important to identify the devices of Satan. It is only when we are aware of his tactics that we can effectively wage war against him. In this section, we will take a look at several common devices of the enemy. As a pastor, I have seen these tactics being employed over and over again by Satan in Christian's lives. I encourage you to carefully examine these devices and prayerfully consider if Satan is waging war against you on these fronts.

# DEVICE #1: UNFORGIVENESS

Unforgiveness is a big hindrance to our relationship with God. Some of us cannot forgive ourselves because Satan reminds us of our past mistakes. Or maybe we hold grudges against those who are responsible for hurts in our past. Whatever the case, unforgiveness is a tool that Satan uses to keep us separated from ourselves, others, and, most importantly, God.

You see, if we do not forgive ourselves, then we will most likely not reach full repentance; and if we do not repent, then God cannot forgive us. At the same time, if we do not forgive our brother's trespasses, we are not in a position to receive full forgiveness and healing from God. (See Matthew 18:35.)

God gives us authority to release ourselves and others from the bondage of unforgiveness. *"Whatever you bind on earth will be bound in heaven, and whatever you loose on earth will be loosed in heaven"* (Matthew 18:18). It is crucial, as God's children, that we take steps to break these bonds of unforgiveness!

When we don't forgive, we give Satan an "in" to our lives. This "in" provides him with new opportunities to cause strife and dissension between ourselves and other Christians.

> *Now whom you forgive anything, I also forgive. For if indeed I have forgiven anything, I have forgiven that one for your sakes in the presence of Christ, lest Satan should take advantage of us; for we are not ignorant of his devices.*
>
> (2 Corinthians 2:10–11)

This is why it is crucial for us to forgive. Do not let the device of unforgiveness creep into your life. Be on the lookout!

# DEVICE #2: PRIDE OF LIFE

What is pride? Pride is puffed-up, all-knowing, self-righteous, and governed by the flesh. Pride is when we are confident that we have everything all figured out when, in reality, we are following foolish human "wisdom." *"There is a way that seems right to a man, but its end is the way of death"* (Proverbs 14:12).

Pride almost always comes before a fall. Many civilizations have collapsed because of pride. Many homes have been broken because of pride. Many souls have been lost because of pride. As Proverbs 16:18 explains, *"Pride goes before destruction, And a haughty spirit before a fall."*

Are you living in pride? Pride can be difficult to identify in our own lives, especially since pride, by its very nature, makes us susceptible to overlooking our faults. One way to check your pride-level, however, is to ask yourself the following questions. Answer them honestly and prayerfully!

1. Can I be corrected or admonished?

2. Can I listen and learn from someone else?

3. Do I look down on people of low estate?

4. Do I try to keep up with the Joneses?

5. Do I do whatever it takes to have fame, fortune, or popularity?

Pride doesn't have to be a bad thing. There is such a thing as good pride. Where many have fallen, however, is in the vanity of their minds. Their understanding has been darkened so that their pride is entirely self-centered. When they take pride in their families, their talents, and their accomplishments, for instance, they forget to give credit to the Lord, the One who has provided them with their families, talents, and accomplishments!

If you're struggling with pride, pray about it. Take time to pinpoint the areas of your life in which you are susceptible to pride. As you identify these areas, start chiseling away at your pride by returning thanks to the Lord, the One who provided all your blessings in the first place.

# DEVICE #3: LUST OF THE FLESH

Just because it sounds good, feels good, and tastes good doesn't mean it's right. Just because everyone else is doing it doesn't mean you should. It is very easy to succumb to the ways of the world, to compromise our standards until our lives are characterized by the lusts of the flesh. As Christians, however, we are called to something higher.

What is lust of the flesh? I like to define it as those things that satisfy our natural man but bring sickness to our spirit man. Galatians 5:19-21 provides several examples of lustful, fleshly behavior:

> *Now the works of the flesh are evident, which are: adultery, fornication, uncleanness, lewdness, idolatry, sorcery, hatred, contentions, jealousies, outbursts of wrath, selfish ambitions, dissensions, heresies, envy, murders, drunkenness, revelries, and the like; of which I tell you beforehand, just as I also told you in time past, that those who practice such things will not inherit the kingdom of God.* (Galatians 5:19-20)

Are you walking in the flesh? Look through the following list. If the following attitudes or behaviors characterize your life, you may be walking in the flesh.

1. I don't have a clear conscience. I feel regretful, ashamed, and/or guilty.

2. I rationalize, justify, and make excuses.

3. I cover up, hide, pretend, and remain in a state of denial.

4. I pilfer, lie, and deceive.

How do we escape the flesh? The truth is that we cannot fully do so until the Lord perfects us completely when we pass from this life to the next. In the meantime, though, we are called to fight against the flesh by walking in the spirit:

> *For though we walk in the flesh, we do not war according to the flesh. For the weapons of our warfare are not carnal but mighty in God for pulling down strongholds, casting down arguments and every high thing that exalts itself against the knowledge of God, bringing every thought into captivity to the obedience of Christ, and being ready to punish all disobedience when your obedience is fulfilled.* (2 Corinthians 10:3–6)

# Appendix B

# Scriptures on Satan

Second Timothy 2:15 says, *"Be diligent to present yourself approved to God, a worker who does not need to be ashamed, rightly dividing the word of truth."* It is sad but true that, these days, we have are often "too busy" to study God's Word on a daily basis. *"The cares of this world and the deceitfulness of riches choke the word"* (Matthew 13:22), so that when affliction or persecution arises, we are easily knocked down and left defenseless against Satan's craftiness.

As believers, it is essential that we equip ourselves with knowledge for defeating Satan and his armies. The source of such knowledge is found only in our Lord's precious Word, the Bible. I encourage you to daily seek God out through prayer and careful study of His Word. You will find it truly rewarding, as well as absolutely crucial, if you are to have spiritual victory over Satan.

Below, I have provided a few Scripture passages to get you started. These passages are specifically on Satan and on how to overcome his wiles. I encourage you, however, to be well-read in all areas of Scripture. Read on many different topics, familiarizing yourself with all of Scripture.

# WHAT SCRIPTURE SAYS ABOUT SATAN

He was once a great angel:

*Thus says the Lord GOD: "You were the seal of perfection, full of wisdom and perfect in beauty. You were in Eden, the garden of God; every precious stone was your covering: the sardius, topaz, and diamond, beryl, onyx, and jasper, sapphire, turquoise, and emerald with gold. The workmanship of your timbrels and pipes was prepared for you on the day you were created. You were the anointed cherub who covers; I established you; you were on the holy mountain of God; you walked back and forth in the midst of fiery stones."* (Ezekiel 28:12–14)

He was separated from God because of pride:

*You were perfect in your ways from the day you were created, till iniquity was found in you. By the abundance of your trading you became filled with violence within, and you sinned; therefore I cast you as a profane thing out of the mountain of God; and I destroyed you, O covering cherub, from the midst of the fiery stones. Your heart was lifted up because of your beauty; you corrupted your wisdom for the sake of your splendor; I cast you to the ground, I laid you before kings, that they might gaze at you. You defiled your sanctuaries by the multitude of your iniquities, by the iniquity of your trading; therefore I brought fire from your midst; it devoured you, and I turned you to ashes upon the earth in the sight of all who saw you. All who knew you among the peoples are astonished at you; you have become a horror, and shall be no more forever.*

(Ezekiel 28:15–19)

*Your pomp is brought down to Sheol, and the sound of your stringed instruments; the maggot is spread under you, and worms cover you. How you are fallen from heaven, O Lucifer, son of the morning! How you are cut down to the ground, you who weakened the nations! For you have said in your heart: "I will ascend into heaven, I will exalt my throne above the stars of God; I will also sit on the mount of the congregation on the farthest sides of the north; I will ascend above the heights of the clouds, I will be like the Most High." Yet you shall be brought down to Sheol, to the lowest depths of the Pit.*

(Isaiah 14:11–15)

165

He has a host of fallen angels, or demons, who assist him:

*And war broke out in heaven: Michael and his angels fought with the dragon; and the dragon and his angels fought, but they did not prevail, nor was a place found for them in heaven any longer. So the great dragon was cast out, that serpent of old, called the Devil and Satan, who deceives the whole world; he was cast to the earth, and his angels were cast out with him.*

(Revelation 12:7–9)

He works to deceive God's people:

*Satan himself transforms himself into an angel of light.*
(2 Corinthians 11:14)

*For false christs and false prophets will rise and show great signs and wonders to deceive, if possible, even the elect.* (Matthew 24:24)

*Now the serpent was more cunning than any beast of the field which the LORD God had made. And he said to the woman, "Has God indeed said, 'You shall not eat of every tree of the garden'?...For God knows that in the day you eat of it your eyes will be opened, and you will be like God, knowing good and evil."* (Genesis 3:1, 5)

He can perform signs:

*He performs great signs, so that he even makes fire come down from heaven on the earth in the sight of men.* (Revelation 13:13)

He is a liar:

*He was a murderer from the beginning, and does not stand in the truth, because there is no truth in him. When he speaks a lie, he speaks from his own resources, for he is a liar and the father of it.* (John 8:44)

He is an accuser:

*Then I heard a loud voice saying in heaven, "Now salvation, and strength, and the kingdom of our God, and the power of His Christ have come, for the accuser of our brethren, who accused them before our God day and night, has been cast down."* (Revelation 12:10)

He brings death:

*The thief does not come except to steal, and to kill, and to destroy. I have come that they may have life, and that they may have it more abundantly.* (John 10:10)

He wages war against God's servants:

*It was granted to him to make war with the saints and to overcome them. And authority was given him over every tribe, tongue, and nation.* (Revelation 13:7)

He will not conquer us when the Spirit is our strength:

*Behold, I give you the authority to trample on serpents and scorpions, and over all the power of the enemy, and nothing shall by any means hurt you.* (Luke 10:19)

He will be defeated by God once and for all:

*Then He will also say to those on the left hand, "Depart from Me, you cursed, into the everlasting fire prepared for the devil and his angels."* (Matthew 25:41)

*Then the seventy returned with joy, saying, "Lord, even the demons are subject to us in Your name." And He said to them, "I saw Satan fall like lightning from heaven. Behold, I give you the authority to trample on serpents and scorpions, and over all the power of the enemy, and nothing shall by any means hurt you. Nevertheless do not rejoice in this, that the spirits are subject to you, but rather rejoice because your names are written in heaven."* (Luke 10:17–20)

*Inasmuch then as the children have partaken of flesh and blood, He Himself likewise shared in the same, that through death He might destroy him who had the power of death, that is, the devil, and release those who through fear of death were all their lifetime subject to bondage.* (Hebrews 2:14–15)

*Then I saw an angel coming down from heaven, having the key to the bottomless pit and a great chain in his hand. He laid hold of the dragon, that serpent of old, who is the Devil and Satan, and bound him for a thousand years; and he cast him into the bottomless pit, and shut him up, and set a seal on him, so that he should deceive the nations no more till the thousand years were finished. But after these things he must be released for a little while.* (Revelation 20:1–3)

# WHAT SCRIPTURE SAYS ABOUT RESISTING SATAN

We must be wary of deception:

*Beloved, do not believe every spirit, but test the spirits, whether they are of God; because many false prophets have gone out into the world.* (1 John 4:1)

We must forgive, so as not to give Satan a foothold:

*For if indeed I have forgiven anything, I have forgiven that one for your sakes in the presence of Christ, lest Satan should take advantage of us; for we are not ignorant of his devices.* (2 Corinthians 2:10–11)

*"Be angry, and do not sin": do not let the sun go down on your wrath, nor give place to the devil.* (Ephesians 4:26–27)

We must be on the lookout for attacks:

*Be sober, be vigilant; because your adversary the devil walks about like a roaring lion, seeking whom he may devour. Resist him, steadfast in the faith, knowing that the same sufferings are experienced by your brotherhood in the world.* (1 Peter 5:8–9)

We are to fight by the Spirit, not in the flesh:

*For though we walk in the flesh, we do not war according to the flesh. For the weapons of our warfare are not carnal but mighty in God for pulling down strongholds, casting down arguments and every high thing that exalts itself against the knowledge of God, bringing every thought into captivity to the obedience of Christ, and being ready to punish all disobedience when your obedience is fulfilled.* (2 Corinthians 10:3–6)

*Finally, my brethren, be strong in the Lord and in the power of His might. Put on the whole armor of God, that you may be able to stand against the wiles of the devil. For we do not wrestle against flesh and blood, but against principalities, against powers, against the rulers of the darkness of this age, against spiritual hosts of wickedness in the heavenly places.* (Ephesians 6:10–12)

We are to resist the devil through Scripture:

*Then Jesus was led up by the Spirit into the wilderness to be tempted by the devil. And when He had fasted forty days and forty nights, afterward He was hungry. Now when the tempter came to Him, he said, "If You are the Son of God, command that these stones become bread." But He answered and said, "It is written, 'Man shall not live by bread alone, but by every word that proceeds from the mouth of God.'"* (Matthew 4:1–4; see also verses 5–11)

We are to put on the armor of God:

*Therefore take up the whole armor of God, that you may be able to withstand in the evil day, and having done all, to stand. Stand therefore, having girded your waist with truth, having put on the breastplate of righteousness, and having shod your feet with the preparation of the gospel of peace; above all, taking the shield of faith with which you will be able to quench all the fiery darts of the wicked one. And take the helmet of salvation, and the sword of the Spirit, which is the word of God; praying always with all prayer and supplication in the Spirit, being watchful to this end with all perseverance and supplication for all the saints.*

(Ephesians 6:13–18)

We must remember that the Lord has already won the battle and defeated Satan:

*You are of God, little children, and have overcome them, because He who is in you is greater than he who is in the world.* (1 John 4:4)

We must remember that Satan is subject to the Lord and His commands:

*...which He worked in Christ when He raised Him from the dead and seated Him at His right hand in the heavenly places, far above all principality and power and might and dominion, and every name that is named, not only in this age but also in that which is to come.*

(Ephesians 1:20–21)

*For I am persuaded that neither death nor life, nor angels nor principalities nor powers, nor things present nor things to come, nor height nor depth, nor any other created thing, shall be able to separate us from the love of God which is in Christ Jesus our Lord.*

(Romans 8:38–39)

# Study and
# Discussion Guide

# Study and Discussion Guide

## Chapter One

1. Lucifer was the anointed and brilliant cherub of God. What was it that separated him from the worship of God?

2. Lucifer made several "I will" statements in Isaiah 14:13–14. Man was infected with the same self-will that separated Lucifer from God. What "I will" statements have you made in your life? These are the things that you decided to do without submitting them first to God. List them here. What were some of the outcomes of those decisions?

3. How is Satan like a jealous woman?

4. Where did Satan get his power from? Why does he continue to possess that power?

5. Explain how Satan is like someone contesting a will.

# Chapter Two

1. What do you think of when you think of witchcraft? How has your view of witchcraft changed since reading this chapter?

2. What is Satan's chief motive in the use of witchcraft? What is he trying to accomplish?

3. In what ways has witchcraft crept into the modern-day church?

4. Second Kings 17:33 tells us that Israel feared God yet at the same time served idols. We sometimes place our confidence in things other than God. Money would be one example. What things have you trusted in or served other than God? List them here.

5. According to George Bloomer, what is religion? How can it become an obstacle?

6. In 1 Samuel 15:22–23, the prophet Samuel told Saul that God was displeased with him. What did he tell Saul is better than sacrifice?

7. State in your own words what you think God is saying in 1 Samuel 15:22.

8. What are the three basic points of Satan's strategy?

# Chapter Three

1.  What is a terrorist? What is his objective?

2.  What effect does fear have on our ability to move into the promises of God?

3.  Describe here any situation in which you were intimidated and stopped short of some blessing. Can you determine exactly what fear intimidated you? (Example: fear of failure, fear of the unknown, etc.)

4.  In the Bible, how did God deal with the fear some of His servants faced?

5.  The enemy uses fear to discourage you from receiving God's inheritance. How might knowing this fact change your attitude the next time you encounter intimidation?

6.  How can we turn the tables on terrorism?

7.  Who is worthy of fear? Who isn't?

8.  How should remembering that it is God who is fighting the battle change the way we look at and approach the war against Satan?

# Chapter Four

1. What is the enemy trying to create in our minds through manipulation, or psychological warfare? What end does he hope to reach by this means?

2. What are some of the forms that "arguments" take in the body of Christ? Describe how you may have allowed the enemy to gain access to your own church.

3. Can you think of a time when things were going well spiritually and a word or thought came along to derail you? Describe what happened. How could you have turned the tables on the enemy's attack?

4.  What does pride do to a person's outlook and behavior? What does it result in?

5.  How is it possible for born-again believers to be troubled by the demonic? Where are the strongholds that we must tear down?

6.  According to John 8:30–32, what are the steps necessary to become free? (Hint: There are four steps.) List them here.

# Chapter Five

1. Describe Satan's tactic of overwhelming force, or domination, and how it works through us.

2. Three things are listed in 1 John 2:16 through which the enemy can distract us from God. What are they, and where else are they mentioned in the Bible?

3. How does an emotional wound result in our trying to dominate another person?

4. What does it mean to walk and live by the Spirit?

5. How is God's love unique? How should its unique quality affect the way we live?

6. How is humility often misunderstood? What is its true meaning?

# Chapter Six

1. What is the most important key in dealing with the enemy?

2. What do both our salvation and our warfare against the enemy depend upon?

3. List the three articles of God's armor that we must *"put on."*

4. List three articles of God's armor that we must *"take up."*

5. Jesus could have chosen to defeat Satan in the wilderness by calling upon his many legions of angels. What did He use instead to defeat the enemy? What does this teach us?

6. What was Paul referring to when he wrote about the helmet of salvation? What happens when we take it up?

7. Why does God give us discernment? How does it work and in what ways can we use it?

8. Describe in a few sentences the differences between the way God speaks and the way the enemy speaks.

# Chapter Seven

1. Who brings us into battle with the enemy?

2. What happens as we grow and learn new levels in God?

3. Have you seen God win battles in your life and church? What were they? How did He show His strength and power?

4. Why can you oppose the workings of evil with confidence?

5.  How might the stories you have read in this chapter change the way you view and approach the enemy?

# Chapter Eight

1.  Where is the war against the enemy ultimately won? Why is it important to know that?

2.  What did the high priest's filthy garments represent? What did the Lord order done with them?

3.  What does it mean to you to know that it was God who ordered that clean robes be put on you?

4.  Are there any areas in your life where you are still trying to save yourself, or to be good enough? If so, list them here, then give them over to God.

5. What does it mean to "walk in God's ways"?

6. What does it mean to "keep God's command"?

7. What one word summarizes Zechariah 3:7? How is it a perfect summary?

# Answer Key

# Answer Key

## Chapter One

1. Lucifer was separated from the worship of God when he began to focus on his own beauty. He allowed pride to take over, causing him to desire worship for himself rather than worship for God.

2. Answers will vary.

3. Satan is like a jealous woman in that he hates to see the loving relationship between God and His saints. The thought of God's creation enjoying any part of what Satan once enjoyed himself deeply angers him. So, like a jealous woman trying to rip apart a relationship that she wishes she could have, Satan seeks to destroy the love and fellowship God has with His saints.

4. Satan got his power from God Almighty. Satan continues to possess that power because God allows him to in order to show us the difference between good and evil.

5. Satan is like someone contesting a will in that he has contested the inheritance of salvation God has left for us. As a result, it looks as though Satan may have power over us; it looks as though he might win the case. But he does not have true power, and Jesus, our advocate and the only one with true power, will take our case and win it with a few drops of His blood if we ask Him to.

## Chapter Two

1. Answers will vary.

2. Through witchcraft, Satan hopes to fulfill his age-old motive: to divert people from God and His truth.

3. Witchcraft has crept into the modern-day church in many ways, including a) through the celebration of Kwanza, which is supposed to be a celebration of African culture but is also filled with spiritism and demonic influence; and b) through the materialism practiced by preachers who wear expensive suits and drive sixty-thousand-dollar cars, causing us to measure our success in terms of facilities and dollars.

4. Answers will vary.

5. Religion, according to George Bloomer, is a system of beliefs about God. Religion can become an obstacle if we begin to relate to our system of beliefs or doctrine and forget about our personal relationship with God.

6. Samuel told Saul that obedience is better than sacrifice.

7. Answers will vary.

8. The three basic points of Satan's strategy are intimidation, manipulation, and domination.

## Chapter Three

1. A terrorist is a coward serving a lost cause by committing heinous acts. Terrorists do not have the power or ability to win an outright confrontation, so they resort to terrorism to prove a point and get some attention. A terrorist's chief objective is to put terror and fear into people.

2. Fear distracts us from God. It causes us to turn away from God's promises and back to bondage like the Israelites did.

3. Answers will vary.

4. God dealt with the fear His servants faced by telling them right from the beginning not to be afraid because He would be with them.

5. Answers will vary.

6. We can turn the tables on terrorism by learning about fear and how the enemy uses it. We can fight terror with focus on God's purpose, fellowship with believers, and facts from God's Word.

7. God alone is worthy of fear; Satan is not.

8. Answers will vary.

# Chapter Four

1. Through manipulation, or psychological warfare, the enemy tries to create doubt in our minds. He does this in order to distract us from God and His truth.

2. Some of the forms that "arguments" take in the body of Christ include criticism, gossip, innuendo, sarcasm, moodiness, and religious pretense.

3. Answers will vary.

4. Pride causes a person to believe that he is above others. It causes him to hold "lesser" people and opinions in contempt. The result of pride is separation and persecution of those we value less.

5. Born-again believers can be troubled by the demonic because strongholds are in the mind, not the spirit, of a believer. When we come to Christ, we are His; however, our minds have not caught up to our spirits. Thus, there is a war being waged in our minds to see who will control it, God or flesh and the devil.

6. According to John 8:30-32, the steps necessary to become free are: 1) Putting your faith in Jesus; 2) holding to Jesus' teaching; 3) being Jesus' disciple; and 4) knowing the truth.

# Chapter Five

1. Satan's tactic of domination consists of overpowering his victim through brute force in an attempt to crush him. If Satan

succeeds in this effort, the crushed person becomes a tool in the hand of Satan to crush and dominate others, keeping them from the grace of God.

2. The three things listed in 1 John 2:16 through which the enemy can distract us from God are: 1) *"the lust of the flesh"*; 2) *"the lust of the eyes"*; and 3) *"the pride of life."* Scripture shows that the devil often attacks each of these areas (flesh, mind, and pride) in succession. This can be seen in the temptation of Eve in Genesis 3:6 and in the temptation of Jesus in Luke 4:3-9.

3. An emotional wound results in our trying to dominate someone because, when we are wounded, our flesh is offended, our mind is distracted, and our pride takes over. We feel that we have a right to judge the one who has wounded us.

4. To walk and live by the Spirit is to live with eyes lifted toward heaven. It involves walking as Jesus did and making pleasing the Father our priority. When we walk by the Spirit we do not walk independently, but we take each step in the footprints of God's leading.

5. God's love is unique in that it is more than a mere emotion; it is a conscious decision. This fact should affect the way we live because we know God will always love us no matter what. It should cause us to set out each day determined to love regardless of the events and people we encounter. It should predispose us toward an attitude of love.

6. Humility has often been misunderstood in that many believe that in order to be humble you must be a doormat. However, to have true humility means that you have a proper concept of God and your relationship to Him.

# Chapter Six

1. The most important key in dealing with the enemy is to depend on the Lord rather than on our own ability to defeat or outsmart Satan. It is by the grace of God alone that Satan is defeated.

2. Both our salvation and our warfare against the enemy depend upon the grace of God through Jesus Christ.

3. We must *"put on"* the truth, righteousness, and peace of Christ.

4. We must *"take up"* the shield of faith, the helmet of salvation, and the sword of the Word.

5. Instead of calling on His legions of angels to defeat Satan in the wilderness, Jesus overcame him with the truth of God's Word. This teaches us the power of Scripture and that we can overcome Satan with God's Word.

6. When Paul spoke about putting on the helmet of salvation, he was referring to protecting our minds. When we take up the helmet of salvation, we are filling our minds with the hope that it is God's intention to redeem and save people everywhere.

7. Discernment is that "God part" of us that warns us when we come into a demonic setting. God gives us discernment so that we can participate in those things that are of God and avoid the snares of the devil. With discernment, the children of God are able to sense God's truth versus Satan's counterfeit and thus give no offense to God.

8. We can differentiate between what is from God and what is from the enemy by observing the attitude or direction of the words or thoughts involved. When the enemy is at work, we feel pushed, panicked, confused, condemned, insecure, and

powerless. When God is at work, we feel invited, peaceful, clear, confronted, loved, and confident.

# Chapter Seven

1. God brings us into battle with the enemy.
2. As we grow and learn new levels in God, we also will encounter new resistance.
3. Answers will vary.
4. You can oppose the workings of evil with confidence because God's faithfulness and ability in battle have been proven throughout the ages. Our power comes from Him, an unlimited and all-powerful source, and with Him we cannot be defeated.
5. Answers will vary.

# Chapter Eight

1. The war against the enemy is ultimately won at the throne of God. Knowing this is important because it means our victory is by God's sovereign grace. Regardless of our efforts or obedience, our restoration is the product of God's love and compassion.
2. The high priest's filthy garments represent the iniquity that separates man from God. Each stain represents a step off the path of God's ways. Showing His grace and mercy, the Lord ordered these filthy garments to be taken away and replaced with rich robes.
3. Answers will vary, but should include something to the effect that because it is God who covers us, we cannot take any credit for our salvation. It is not by our effort or perfection that we stand in God's presence; it is by His decision

alone. We are clothed with His righteousness simply because He loves us.

4. Answers will vary.

5. To "walk in God's ways" means to live a "throne-ward" life. It means living to please and glorify God. It means making God the focus of all you do rather than a sentimental afterthought.

6. To "keep God's command" is to live a life of listening to God and responding in obedience. It also requires that we live in a dynamic relationship with God. God is always speaking and always moving, so we must always be listening and responding to what we hear.

7. The one word that summarizes Zechariah 3:7 is *access*. This word is a perfect summary because this verse states that we have access to God and that we can walk in His very presence.

# About the Author

# About the Author

Bishop George G. Bloomer is a native of Brooklyn, New York. After serving as an evangelist for fourteen years, Dr. Bloomer began pastoring in 1996. He is the founder and senior pastor of Bethel Family Worship Center in Durham, North Carolina, but continues to travel extensively, sharing with others his testimony of how the Lord delivered him from a life of poverty, drug abuse, sexual abuse, and mental anguish. "God had a plan for my life," Bloomer now says, "and even during my span of lawlessness, the angels of the Lord were protecting me because the call of God was upon my life."

Bloomer holds the degree of doctor of religious arts in Christian psychology and conducts many seminars dealing with relationships, finances, and stress management. He is founder of Young Witnesses for Christ, a youth evangelistic outreach ministry with several chapters on college campuses throughout the United States, and bishop of C.L.U.R.T (Come Let Us Reason Together) International Assemblies, comprised of over eighty churches nationwide and abroad. His message is one of deliverance and of a hope that far exceeds the desperation and oppression of many silent sufferers.

# OTHER BOOKS BY GEORGE BLOOMER...

*Authority Abusers*

*Crazy House, Sane House* (with Jeannie Bloomer)

*Empowered from Above*

*When Loving You Is Wrong*

# AUDIO CDS BY GEORGE BLOOMER...

*Apples and Oranges*

*I Had a Dream*

*It's a Beautiful Day*

*Now That the Raven Has Gone*

*When God Reveals Himself*

*10 Stupid Things Women Do to Mess Up Their Lives*

*Songs of Jabez*

*Spiritual Authority Series*

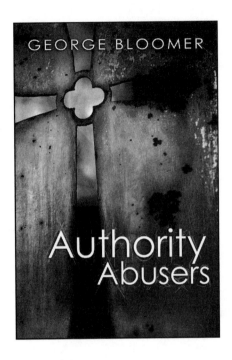

## Authority Abusers

*George Bloomer*

As surely as the absence of authority produces chaos, the abuse of
authority produces destruction. Tragically, it's inside the church—
where salvation and love should abound—that some of the worst
authority abuse takes place. God's design for authority has been
misunderstood, twisted, and manipulated, leaving the innocent as
victims and prisoners of controlling situations. Wake up! This is
not God's design for the church—or for authority. Discover the
key to breaking free from the bondage of spiritual abuse.

ISBN: 0-88368-768-2 • Trade • 160 pages

**tʊ**
WHITAKER
HOUSE
**Flooding the World with the Gospel**
Visit our website at: www.whitakerhouse.com

## Empowered from Above
*George Bloomer*

Are you walking in power as Christ did? Is your desire for intimacy with the Father increasing? Are you passionately pursuing the Holy Spirit's presence? Prepare to discover a deeper understanding of the indwelling of the Spirit. Join Bishop George G. Bloomer as he provides solid, scriptural answers on the Holy Spirit—His person, His fruits, His gifts, His unifying work. There's no need to be pulled apart in a doctrinal tug-of-war or to live in confusion any longer. As you begin to walk in this deeper understanding, you will be filled with new wisdom, power, and strength. Prepare to be *Empowered from Above*.

ISBN: 0-88368-285-0 • Trade • 160 pages

**Flooding the World with the Gospel**
WHITAKER HOUSE
Visit our website at: www.whitakerhouse.com

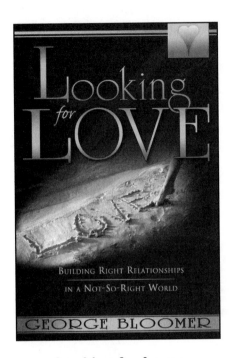

## Looking for Love:
## Building Right Relationships in a Not-So-Right World
## (with CD)
*George Bloomer*

Deep down, each of us wants to experience a relationship that will give us the love, support, and intimate friendship we so desperately desire. If you're ready to discover the essential keys to experiencing lasting love, then let George Bloomer show you the way to establishing godly relationships that will stand the test of time. Whether you're married or still looking for that special someone, find out how to develop deeper intimacy by growing closer to God. Then start enjoying loving, lasting relationships far beyond all you could ever ask or imagine!

ISBN: 0-88368-991-X • Trade with CD • 176 pages

**W** WHITAKER HOUSE  **Flooding the World with the Gospel**  Visit our website at: www.whitakerhouse.com

## Crazy House, Sane House
*George and Jeannie Bloomer*

She's not the same woman you married. He's not the man you thought he was. This is nothing like you imagined it would be. Sometimes in a marriage relationship, things can get crazy and out of control. The decisions made in those times determine the strength of the household you build. Whether wedding bells are in your near future or you have been married for decades, you can begin to reconstruct the building blocks that will put sanity and stability into the foundation of your relationship. Discover the keys to building a strong house, a strong marriage, and a strong future. Crazy house or sane house—the choice is yours!

ISBN: 0-88368-726-7 • Trade • 144 pages

WHITAKER HOUSE — Flooding the World with the Gospel
Visit our website at: www.whitakerhouse.com

# Spiritual Authority Series (5 CD Set)

*George Bloomer*

Authority—at its best, it's a blessing, a representation of the Lord's gracious guidance and leading of His sheep. However, when tainted by sin and selfishness, authority can turn into a curse. It doesn't matter where this authority comes into play—the classroom, the church, the home, or the workplace. What matters is that God-given authority is in alignment with the Lord's perfect provision for leadership. In this dynamic series, Bishop George Bloomer explores principles that can ensure the proper exercise of authority in every area of our lives.

ISBN: 0-88368-966-9 • 5 CDs • UPC: 6-30809-68967-2
(The CDs in this set are also available individually.)

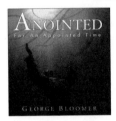

## Anointed for an Appointed Time
ISBN: 0-88368-967-7 • CD • UPC: 6-30809-68967-2

## Departing Spirits
ISBN: 0-88368-969-3 • CD • UPC: 6-30809-68969-6

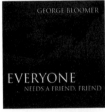

## Everyone Needs a Friend, Friend
ISBN: 0-88368-968-5 • CD • UPC: 6-30809-68968-9

## Witchcraft in the Pews
ISBN: 0-88368-970-7 • CD • UPC: 6-30809-68970-2

## Witchcraft in the Pulpit
ISBN: 0-88368-971-5 • CD • UPC: 6-30809-68971-9

**WHITAKER HOUSE**   **Flooding the World with the Gospel**
Visit our website at: www.whitakerhouse.com